Elections, Conventions, The Presidency, Congress, and Supreme Court Explained

The Quick and Dirty Guide to Our Messy Democracy
Volumes 1-4

By Chris Bartlett

Printed in the United States of America

First Printing, 2016

It's the Journey not the Destination LLC

　　PO Box 350457

　　Westminster CO 80035-0457

　　www.thequickanddirtyguide.com

Table of Contents

Volume One: The Quick and Dirty Guide to Primaries Caucuses and Political Conventions

It is an American media tradition to claim that whatever election is happening at the time is unlike any other in history. Usually this is just media hype. Every election is unique in some ways. The election of 1992 gave America the first credible three candidate race since 1912. 2008 presented America with the chance to elect its first minority President or its first veteran of Vietnam. It was also America's first chance in 24 years to have a Presidential ballot without the names "Bush" or "Clinton" on it. 2012 gave America the opportunity to roll back universal health care and elect the first Mormon to the Oval Office. America declined to do either but it we still had the opportunity to.

However, the current election's claim to the "once in a lifetime" title rests on more secure ground than many of its predecessors. America has the opportunity to choose between a reality TV star with no experience in government and who lacks the support of much of his political party, a woman who is the former First Lady and is being investigated by the FBI, a Jewish man who wears the label of "socialist" proudly, and an Hispanic who is reviled by much of his own party. There's also a long shot of a conservative white governor taking the Republican nomination, but that would not be as interesting

America's process of choosing a nominee allows for political newbies and radicals to make their case to the people about why they should become the most powerful person on Earth. It is in tune with America's aspirations about being a land of opportunity. While plenty of people (including the establishments of both major parties) might not like that the opportunity for an untested outsider like billionaire Donald Trump to become President exists, one cannot deny that it is exciting.

As of the writing of this book in April of 2016, it is still unknown who the major party nominees will be. America is still in the midst of its primaries and caucuses, the results of which will only be known at the Republican and Democratic conventions in July. While other political parties in other countries also have primary elections, few are as chaotic as those in America. Fewer still leave the possibility open that someone with no political experience and without the support of party leadership could seize the nomination.

This book will shed light on this arcane and occasionally non-sensical nominating process. We'll check out the differences between primaries and caucuses, and how differently the two parties have organized them. From there we will move on to the national conventions where, regardless of the primary and caucus results, the leadership of the political parties may choose to reinterpret the nominating rules even after the voters have spoken.

Due to the chaotic nature of primary season it is possible that this book could be outdated within a week of its publication. Fortunately the kindle format allows for frequent updates. The Quick and Dirty Guide Team will endeavor to keep it updated but we hope you'll forgive us if events overtake our ability to modify the text on the ebook version of this text.

Chapter One: Primaries and Caucuses

The nomination process of 2016 has lasted longer than many election campaigns. The American media have spent time and money trying to explain the process to the citizens, but much of this information has been marred by its partisan nature. News corporations now battle for ratings and advertising dollars rather than clarity of presentation, barely attempting to hide which party they prefer. It's the ordinary citizen who relies upon the media for understanding and clarification that suffers because of these faults.

The primary and caucus systems themselves are also to blame for these misunderstandings. These are archaic systems that have evolved from a time when party leaders would travel by horse and carriage to decide upon a candidate. It is because of these roots that primaries and caucuses don't actually choose the nominees, but rather contribute to the decision of who will represent a state party at the national party's convention.

You are not alone if you didn't follow all of that. Let's pull back. Each of the fifty states has a state Democratic Party and a state Republican Party. The state primaries or caucuses allow the state parties to come together and decide which candidate the party delegations will support at the national party conventions.

To make matters more complicated, those delegates don't always have to vote for the candidate that their state's voters chose. Most state delegates are "bound" to vote for whomever the voters chose but under certain circumstances they can shift their support to another candidate. Republican state parties in particular have wildly divergent guidelines on how binding a primary or caucus result may be on a delegate. This makes final delegate selection crucial for Republican candidates, particularly in a close race.

The final delegate selection for a state occurs at the state party convention; these occur after that state's caucus/primary but before the national party convention. Many of the delegates chosen at these events have instructions to support the candidates who received a significant amount of votes statewide or a candidate who won a plurality of votes in a congressional district. The specifics vary from state to state. These delegates are bound to support the candidate that reflects the will of the voters but in the event that the candidate leaves the race or if the nominating convention has multiple rounds of voting without selecting a nominee they may switch their support to another candidate.

Different states have different rules regarding when a delegate is "released" to vote for a different candidate but these rules allow for delegates to use their best judgment on selecting a nominee that represents the will of the voters but also contributes to the long-term well being of the party and country. Because of these responsibilities the state officials who choose delegates for the national convention do so with an eye on picking people who can be trusted to change their votes to a unifying candidate if the situation demands it.

For a current example, one can look at the Cruz campaigns efforts in Louisiana. Even though he did not win the primary there, his campaign has made sure that the delegates to the national convention are favorable to his campaign. Many of those delegates will have to support Donald Trump at the convention at first, but if Trump fails to secure a majority of delegate votes on the first ballot (contested conventions will be explained below), those delegates can switch their support to Ted Cruz on the next ballot; the way the people vote in the caucuses and primaries matter but they are not always the final word. State party officials and the arm-twisting abilities of campaign staffers may matter even more.

As if that wasn't enough, the Democrats have "Superdelegates" who can vote for whatever candidate they wish to, regardless of how their home state voted. Superdelegates comprise about 15% of the total delegates, more than enough to influence a close race. Democratic superdelegates are members of the party apparatus: former Presidents, congressmen, governors, and state party officials.

Republicans have superdelegates as well, but they are much less powerful than the Democratic equivalent. In fact, we should just call them "delegates." Each state has three and they are required to vote in line with the results of their state's primary or caucus. These rules were updated in 2012 with the idea of preventing an insurgent candidate (Rob Paul in 2012) from gaining delegate support. Ironically, those rules are now constraining the Republican Party leadership from preventing the nomination of Donald Trump. The intricacies of delegate selection make it important to remember that the Political Parties are not government organizations; a delegate who defects from one candidate to another risks being punished by the party but has not broken any laws.

Primaries

Primaries are not simple affairs but they are more straightforward than a caucus. In a primary election, people cast their votes on secret ballots. The party keeps a record of who voted, but nobody knows whom an individual actually voted for. While every state has its own quirks, primaries can be divided into two major categories: open and closed.

All voters can participate in an open primary regardless of their party affiliation. This can lead to a variety of shenanigans. One form of these shenanigans is "raiding." This is when voters from one party "cross the aisle" to vote in the primary of another party. While it is possible that these raiders do this because they are keeping an open mind and are interested in the other party's candidate, this is most likely used to get the opposing party to choose a candidate that they want their own party's candidate to run against. Raiders would hope to get the other party to nominate a flawed candidate who might be easier to beat in the national election.

Open primaries are used in 21 states. Here's a list for you trivia buffs/wannabe Raiders: Alabama, Alaska, Arkansas, Georgia, Hawaii, Indiana, Michigan, Minnesota, Mississippi, Missouri, Montana, North Dakota, Ohio, South Carolina, South Dakota, Tennessee, Texas, Utah, Vermont, Virginia, and Wisconsin.

A closed primary is only open to registered members of a political party, and many states require a voter to have been registered with that political party for a period of time before the primary occurs to prevent the raiding shenanigans described above. Because of the New York Republican Party requiring primary voters to be registered Republicans for at least a year before the voting, Donald Trump's children were unable to support him in the April 19th primary. Closed elections tend to favor candidates that are more in line with the party leadership as registered independents or members of a third party cannot influence the result.

Closed primaries occur in fifteen states. They are Connecticut, Delaware, Florida, Kentucky, Maine, Nebraska, Nevada, New Jersey, New Mexico, New York, Oklahoma, Ohio, Oregon, and Pennsylvania.

The final form of the primary is the exotically named "nonpartisan blanket primary," also known as the "jungle primary." This does not impact Presidential primaries but it can throw a wrench in the election plans of a potential governor or senator. In a jungle primary, all the candidates from every party are one ballot and are voted for all at once. The top two candidates then proceed to the general election. This can lead to two candidates for governor being from the same political party. The states that use this system, and each of them vary in specifics, are Louisiana, California, and Washington.

When it comes to appointing delegates based upon the vote count, Republicans are more complicated than Democrats. In a Democratic primary, delegates are awarded proportionately: if one candidate gets 55% of the vote, then they get 55% of the available state delegates. In most states there is a requirement for a candidate to receive at least 15% of the vote to be awarded any delegates; this prevents fringe candidates from amassing a large enough number of delegates to be influential at the convention.

Republican primaries vary between (and can combine) a proportional system based upon how a whole state voted, a system whereby the winners of congressional districts receive delegates, and a "winner-take-all" system. In 2016, any state holding a primary or caucus before March 15th had to award delegates proportionally, but after March 15 they are allowed to use the winner-take-all model. Some states also have greater weight because of loyalty; states with Republican governors or Republican majority legislatures have more delegates. This allows voters in states that are more likely to vote Republican in the general election to have a larger influence on who the nominee will be. For example, reliably Republican Oklahoma has 15 more delegates than liberal Oregon does despite both states having about 4 million residents.

Additionally, some states apportion delegates based upon which candidates won specific congressional districts. This prevents a candidate from spending all of their time in a heavily populated urban area while ignoring rural communities.

As an example let's take a look at the delegate selection results from above mentioned Louisiana. This state has 46 delegates. 18 of these delegates are district based; three delegates from each of the state's six Congressional Districts are proportionally allocated to the Presidential candidates according to the proportional results of the primary votes in each Congressional District. Of the remaining 28 delegates three are from the Republican National Committee and will vote for the statewide primary winner. Ten of them are "at-large delegates" and 15 are "bonus delegates" (these delegates are given to Louisiana as a reward for its loyal Republican voting record) and are allocated in proportion to the total statewide vote but only candidates who win more than 20% of the vote receive any delegates from this group.

The six congressional districts all spread their votes nearly evenly between Trump, Cruz, and Rubio; in five out of six districts each of these three candidates received enough votes to be awarded one delegate each. Only one district differed in these results, awarding one delegate to Trump and two delegates to Cruz and none to Rubio. The statewide popular vote was split between Trump at

41% and Cruz at 38% with no other candidate breaking the 20% minimum to receive an at-large delegate, this resulted in Trump gaining 12 delegates and Cruz receiving 11. The final result is that the Louisiana delegation will have 18 delegates bound to Trump, 18 bound to Cruz, and the five delegates Marco Rubio won from Congressional districts are unbound now that he has exited the race (more on the impact lasting influence of Senator Rubio in the Convention section of the book.)

Caucuses

You have probably done the math and realized that the majority of states use primaries to choose candidates. While the primaries are relatively straight forward, the caucuses were designed in an America that was even less insistent on the principle of "One person, one vote" than the country we have now.

Instead of going to a voting station and casting a ballot, voters attend private events run by the state political parties. These are often held in school gymnasiums, churches, or other meeting places that can hold a few hundred dedicated caucus goers.

Like a closed primary, only registered party members can participate in a caucus. A caucus can also take a whole day so it can attract more passionate, and often more politically radical, people than a primary. This is even truer at caucuses for the Democrats than the Republicans. Republican caucuses use a secret ballot while Democrats show support for their candidates by raising hands or clustering into groups to be counted. Democratic caucuses can go on for hours before a candidate is chosen. The potential length of these events has been criticized as disenfranchising people who cannot afford to give an entire evening to the party, namely parents without a babysitter or those who can't get off work. This has led one group of Democrats to have a stronger voice at a caucus then their numbers would show in a primary: college students. These passionate and energetic students have been cited as a reason for President Obama's early caucus victories over Hillary Clinton in 2008 and for Bernie Sanders strength in caucus contests in 2016.

A Democratic state caucus is an exciting affair. In Iowa when it is time for a vote, the caucus goers break into groups that support each candidate. If a candidate fails to get at least 15% of the caucus goers to support them, then that candidate is eliminated and his/her supporters can move into other groups for the next vote. This process continues until there are no candidates with less than 15% of the vote. In between votes, the supporters of successful candidates argue with each other and try to convince people to switch support from one candidate to another. The ability for neighbors and coworkers to see which candidate another person supports (and voice their opinion on that choice) have been cited as another element of the Democratic caucus system that can lead to skewed results.

Democratic caucuses award delegates in proportion to the statewide vote. Republican caucuses can use a statewide proportional system, a system based upon who won the Congressional Districts, or a mixture of the two.

Why Iowa?

Iowa has come up several times so far because it holds the first caucus or primary in the country for both parties. Why does this one state, which has less than 1% of the country's population, which is 94% white, and completely lacking in major league sports teams get to give the first official opinion on who should run for President? The answer is simply "tradition." As regular voters began to have more influence over the nomination process in the 1970's, the Iowa Democrats scheduled their caucuses first. Four years later the Iowa Republicans followed suit. Since then Iowa has been the first state to make its opinion known for both parties.

This situation is not without its criticisms. A solid win in Iowa can give a candidate with limited appeal to other parts of the country media attention that they may not have received otherwise. Alternatively, a candidate who under performs in Iowa may appear to be weaker than they actually are. It also cements the governmental influence of lobbies within Iowa who may not have the whole country's best interests at heart. For example, national politicians are slow to ignore the ethanol lobby from Iowa despite it not having a beneficial outcome on the economies of most other states.

Iowa does have a history of influencing the nomination process. Since 1972, Iowa caucuses have had a 50% success rate in predicting the Republican nominee and a 43% success rate for the Democrats. In 2008, President Obama's unexpected victory there set the stage for a protracted battle with Hillary Clinton over who would ultimately seize the nomination.

In 2012, the race for Republican frontrunner in Iowa was between Rick Santorum and Mitt Romney. Romney was originally declared the winner, but in subsequent recounts that took weeks to verify, it was discovered that Santorum had actually narrowly beaten Romney. Of course by the time this was discovered Romney had received the "Iowa Bump" in media attention, won the New Hampshire primary, and was far ahead of Santorum and many other candidates.

Chapter Two: Conventions

If you like spectacle, then you'll love a nominating convention. The political elite from the entire country descends upon the host city of their respective political party. Networks and media firms dedicate 24-hour coverage to the event and hundreds to thousands of protesters usually appear to make sure the political establishment accounts for the protester's positions. In 2016, the Republican convention will be held in Cleveland, Ohio while the Democrats will gather in Philadelphia, Pennsylvania.

The conventions are typically in major cities that can support such a large event. Because of the substantial economic benefits of hosting a convention, cities will compete with each other for the notoriety and the money that comes with hosting a convention. More recently the parties also seem to choose swing states for their convention locations.

Convention locations were originally chosen for practicality's sake. Before air travel made the entire country reachable in five hours, delegates had to travel by horse, carriage, or boat to the convention city. This frequently called for a city somewhere on the mid-Atlantic coast. As railroads became prominent and the American population spread westward, more centralized locations became popular. Chicago, Illinois has held twenty-five major party conventions so far.

The theoretical purpose of conventions is to nominate a Presidential and Vice-Presidential nominee. However, they also serve as a media event to showcase the bright ideas of the party. Party platforms are agreed upon and announced and lip service is paid to groups and factions whose support will be required to win the general election. The media scrutiny of these events has also encouraged political parties to appear as united as possible for the cameras. Because of this, the parties have worked hard for the last few decades to make sure that the nominees for the Presidency and Vice-Presidency were known before the convention. If the party has failed to coalesce around a single set of candidates, then fans of the political drama get what they have always wanted but party leaders have feared: an open convention.

Open, Brokered, or Contested Conventions

An open convention occurs if no Presidential candidate has received a majority of the delegates by the time the event begins. It's difficult to predict what will happen at a contested convention ("open," "brokered," and "contested" are used interchangeably and inconsistently to described a convention that begins without a clear nominee in place.) This is partially because there are few modern historical precedents, but also because the parties can rewrite convention rules before the event even starts. Assuming that none of the Republican candidates has managed to receive a majority of the delegates based upon the primary and caucus results there will undoubtedly be close media scrutiny on Republican leaders like Paul Ryan, Reince Priebus, and Mitch McConnell in the weeks leading up to the convention. These rules can then be accepted or refused by a majority vote of the present delegates.

With the rules for a 2016 contested convention not being set it is difficult to summarize what could occur, but imagining something similar to a caucus puts us on the right track. In this scenario the delegates would cast their ballots for the candidates their parties required them to. The ballots would be counted and if no candidate managed to get a majority of the total national delegates the candidates with fewer delegates would be pressured to drop out of contention, possibly throwing their support behind a candidate with a higher delegate count. This process would repeat itself until one candidate wins the majority of the available delegates. If the parties reach an impasse then it is possible for a person to be nominated that did not run in the primaries and caucuses if enough delegates are in favor of it.

The conventions only require a simple majority for a candidate to be nominated. It does not matter if a candidate has a large plurality coming into the convention; "Candidate A" could receive 45% of the votes on a ballot, "Candidate B" could receive 35%, and "Candidate C" could receive 20%. If the supporters of Candidate A refuse to consider Candidate B but are open to Candidate C, and B's supporters refuse to vote for A but would consider voting for C then Candidate C may well become the nominee. Situations as complicated as this have occurred (see the "Klanbake" in the Convention History section.) Even Abraham Lincoln came in second on the first ballot at the Republican convention of 1860. He went on to cinch the nomination on the third ballot and the two subsequent Presidential elections.

At a contested convention there is also the question of what to do with the delegates assigned to candidates who have withdrawn from the race. The wishes of a defeated candidate generally do not mean much. Once a candidate suspends their campaign it is assumed that the delegates they may have earned in any primaries they participated in are no longer bound to that candidate. Each state party can decide what the delegates who are pledged to a defeated candidate can do. Some states distribute them to the remaining candidates based upon those candidates national vote shares or allow the delegates to vote for whomever they choose. Other states require those delegates to not vote for any other candidate for one or two rounds of voting at the national convention. Still other states require the delegates to stay loyal to the defeated candidate until that candidate "releases" them to vote as they wish. In any of these events, the importance of influencing who is actually filling each delegate role is clear.

These rules are usually an afterthought but, as has been pointed out before, 2016 is like no other year. Prior to suspending his campaign, Marco Rubio collected 169 delegates. Instead of simply allowing the state parties to decide the fate of these positions, Rubio has personally written to the Republican Party heads of each state in which he won delegates and asked them to have the delegates remain "bound" to him until at least the first ballot is cast at the convention. This has never occurred before. If the state party heads agree, then despite exiting the race for President, Senator Rubio may have an enduring influence on the Presidential race.

In most years the Vice Presidential nominee is known before the convention as well. The presumed Presidential nominee will announce their choice for VP and that person will be "affirmed by acclamation" (the convention Chairman says their name and everyone cheers) at the convention. In the event of a brokered convention, there is no way to know how the process will go. One possibility is that one of the candidates with more delegates will ask a candidate with fewer delegates to be the VP nominee in exchange for those delegates' support but there is no modern precedent. It's possible that a convention could conclude without a VP nominee being chosen.

Chapter Three: Historically Significant Conventions

If 2016 does present the country with one or more contested conventions it would not be a complete break from tradition. There have been several conventions where the results were in doubt prior to the event. Some of these conventions will remain historical footnotes while at least one has reverberations to this day.

The 1924 Democratic National Convention in New York City holds the title of "longest continually meeting convention" in American history. It retains the nickname of the "Klanbake." The pun was inspired by the influence of the Klu Klux Klan on the Democratic Party of the time as well as suggestive of how hot the summer was. The Klanbake, which was held at Madison Square Garden from June 24 to July 9th, had a record of 109 rounds of voting to decide upon a presidential nominee.

The convention began with fifteen separate candidates in the race and the party was dealing with the most divisive issue of the day: Prohibition. Tensions also ran high due to racial issues. Some wanted a party platform that denounced the violent actions of extremist groups (clearly targeting the Klu Klux Klan without directly naming it) while the Klan attempted to push its own agenda. In a stunning display of passion, a brawl broke out on the convention floor not merely between delegates and the party faithful but between the governors of Colorado and Kentucky.

This convention is not merely known for its divisiveness. This was also the first convention where a woman, Lena Springs, was on the ballot for the office of Vice President. This convention was also broadcast coast to coast via radio, allowing for Democrats all across the country to be engrossed, enraged, and then exhausted at the party's failure to find unity. A compromise candidate, John W. Davis, was settled upon after it became clear that the front-runners could not unify the party. Mr. Davis went on to be soundly defeated by Republican Calvin Coolidge, 382 electoral votes to 136.

Despite the chaos of the Klanbake, it pales in comparison to the disaster of the Democratic convention of 1968 in Chicago. President Johnson had declined to run for reelection, and the early summer assassinations of Martin Luther King Jr. and Robert Kennedy had been followed by violent riots in more than one hundred American cities.

Over 10,000 demonstrators gathered in Chicago for the convention and were met by 23,000 police and National Guardsmen. The protesters were led by the

National Mobilization Committee to End the War in Vietnam, the Students for a Democratic Society, and the Youth International Party. With tensions inflamed due to the continuing war in Vietnam and America's longstanding racial problems violence broke out on the streets and occasionally in the convention halls.

With the convention being broadcast over television, the rest of America was shocked at the chaos. Using the country's dismay at events in Chicago, Richard Nixon campaigned as the candidate of law and order (an example of historical irony) and went on to defeat the Democratic nominee, Hubert Humphrey, by 110 electoral votes and half a million popular votes. Despite the chaos in Chicago at the time it's worth pointing out that Hubert Humphrey had the nomination before the convention began.

The Republican Party has a history of comparatively sedate conventions. The only convention of note does, however, apply to the 2016 election. In 1976, President Gerald Ford had not secured enough support to win the nomination on the first ballot. Moreover, he was being challenged by Republican rising star and future President, Ronald Reagan. President Ford had managed to win more delegates and votes during the primaries and caucuses, but had not passed that all-important 50% line to have a delegate majority. He was still being criticized within the party due his attempts at détente with the Soviet Union. This combined with the fall of Saigon in 1975 and Ford's unpopular pardoning of Richard Nixon gave cover to those who wanted to replace the President. He had never won a national election in any case as he was appointed to the Vice Presidency after the resignations of Spiro Agnew and then to the Presidency due to the resignation of President Nixon in 1974. To make matters more complicated for the incumbent, Reagan had a national popular vote lead on Ford.

Ford and Reagan arrived in Kansas City attempting to woo the necessary delegates to their side. Reagan was charismatic and passionate while President Ford was still the President and was able to schmooze his way across the finish line. Reagan also cost himself support by inviting a Senator from the party's liberal wing onto his ticket as a Vice-Presidential nominee. Ford won went on lose the election to the former Governor of Georgia, Jimmy Carter, by 57 electoral votes. The Republicans of 2016 should be wary of the above examples; chaotic and contested conventions do not bode well for a party's success in the general election.

America's nomination process suffers from the same handicaps as the Federal government itself. The United States is huge, geographically and demographically, and is as diverse a country as has ever existed. Our divisions can be categorized by political party, religion, economic status, race, ethnicity, gender, opinion about what gender even is, and many other qualities. The founding fathers were acutely aware of the difficulties of governing a vast territory and they were originally considering a country that only hugged the Atlantic seaboard and had 4,000,000 people. Giving 315,000,000 people across a continent sized country a chance to impact not just who the President will be but whom the parties should nominate is an unsurprisingly complicated process.

The length and complexity of the process does allow for many chances for candidates to rise and fall and the voters to have an impact on their fates. Even the methods that the two parties use are reflective of their ideological diversity. The Democrats proportional representation process attempts to give a voter in New York City similar influence to an itinerant beach bum in Hawaii while maintaining a Superdelegate veto power over the voter's final choice. On the other hand the National Republican Party lets the state parties set most of their own rules for how their delegates are assigned and then constrains itself and others to live with the results and perhaps suffer the consequences.

The Primary and Caucus system can be lambasted as many things: too long, too complicated, too expensive, too mysterious, too open to radicals, too beholden to the establishment, too democratic or not democratic enough. This strange mixture however is quintessentially American. A country that sometimes seems cobbled together from people originating all over the world and holding a diverse set of values might need a system that seems cobbled together as well. Regardless of whether or not its a good system it is us up to the American people to change or tolerate it. As H. L. Mencken wrote in 1916, as Woodrow Wilson (who supported American involvement in WWI in 1917) campaigned on a platform of staying out of WWI, "Democracy is the theory that the common people know what they want, and deserve to get it good and hard."

Thank you for reading The Quick and Dirty Guide to Primaries, Caucuses, and Political Conventions. This book began as a series of Google searches to find out what was so super about superdelegates and has blossomed into the first book of the Quick and Dirty Guide to Our Messy Democracy. We hope you enjoyed the book, learned a lot, and will stay with us for our second book: The Quick and Dirty Guide to Electing the President.

Recommended further reading

Chaos: The Outsider's Guide to a Contested Republican National Convention by John Patrick Yob

Primary Politics: Everything You Need to Know about How America Nominates Its Presidential Candidates by Elaine C. Kamarck

http://www.thegreenpapers.com/

Volume Two: The Quick and Dirty Guide to Electing the President

Chapter One: The Office of the President

Before we examine the process to become President we should discuss the responsibilities and powers of the position. That way you are better informed about whether or not this is a job worth pursuing. Initially, the office of the Presidency was established as a counterpoint to the monarchy of Great Britain and as a contrast to monarchies and despotic regimes in general. It should be noted that the monarchy of Britain, by the time of the American Revolution, was not all-powerful. It was constrained by an elected House of Commons in the Parliament, as well as other laws put in place to control the monarch over the centuries. The founders of the United States often used, and referred to the English common laws, the Magna Carta, and British Parliamentary rules and procedures when creating the new United States government. However, the fear of a remote, authoritarian ruler drove the American colonists to craft a unique set of specific duties for the Executive branch of government. As is par for the course in the realm of politics and legal authority, these duties have changed and expanded exponentially over the last 200 plus years.

The original purpose of the office was to serve as a little more than a glorified clerk. The founding fathers were so afraid of creating a new Monarchy that they envisioned a chief executive who was more secretary or administrative assistant than Commander and Chief of any sort. In fact, there were six presidents prior to Washington. These men were elected by the Continental Congress to serve the role of clerk and record keeper. While the American constitution and the republic it created are based on checks of power and the balance thereof, the office of the President was especially limited in its early days.

At the time, the President had no constitutional power to declare war or broker peace. That authority always fell to the Senate, much akin to the way the Roman Republic was designed to work. In fact, the Roman Republic was a widely used template for the formation and functions of the U.S. government. This is one of the many ways the presidential mandate has increased over the decades; many have used the title of "Commander-and-Chief" of the armed forces to send the military wherever they thought needed without having to ask for Congressional approval.

The Constitution does lay out the specific powers of the office, powers that have grown tremendously. The President may convene a special session of Congress "on extraordinary occasions." This most frequently occurs in order to complete unfinished tasks for the year, delays which are usually caused by the conflicts between the Republicans and the Democrats. Important unfinished tasks might include the operating budget for the next fiscal year or legislation of particular importance. Other reasons for convening a special session would be emergencies like war or natural disasters. On the occasion that Congress is unable to adjourn due to ongoing and unresolved debates, the President has the power to send them home.

Much like a Roman Consul or Tribune, the President has the power to *veto* (Latin for *"I forbid"*) legislation. This veto power allows the president to say, "No, this bill shall not become law" to any legislation that Congress passes. However Congress can overturn a Presidential veto. This can only be accomplished with a two-third majority in both the House and Senate. The President also has the power to pardon people for Federal crimes. This pardon power was controversial from the outset. Anti-Federalists remembered examples of royal abuses of the pardon power in Britain, and warned that the same would happen in their new republic. Recently, both Bill Clinton's and George W. Bush's pardons of criminals they were friendly with have drawn intense scrutiny and criticism. The most infamous pardon was Gerald Ford granting Richard Nixon clemency from all prosecutions due to offenses committed during the Watergate scandal. Presidents often use their pardon power on their last days in office, to limit political fallout and media controversy. This strikes some as a cowardly act, others as smart politics.

The President shares two important powers with the Senate. While the President cannot declare war or peace, he can negotiate treaties and ask for a declaration of war. The Senate however must approve these treaties. In addition, the President can appoint federal judges; including the Supreme Court's justices, an issue that has become particularly contentious as of late. He can also appoint other officers of the United States such as Ambassadors, and cabinet posts such as the Secretary of State, Secretary of Defense, the Attorney General and all other cabinet level offices. He can also create special offices like the National Security Director and the Department of Homeland Security. Not to mention he can appoint what are now termed *Czars* to oversee very specific issues like human trafficking, or the Israeli-Palestinian peace process. In addition, the President can appoint the CIA, NSA, and FBI directors as well. Keep in mind all these positions too, are up for review and confirmation by the Senate and many such hearings in recent years have become especially partisan and heated, even for non-political nominees. Partisan senators tend to use the confirmation hearings as a stage to conduct political theater and to espouse party rhetoric.

Most Americans are totally unaware that the President actually has only two constitutional duties. This is hard to fathom given the powers the office has acquired since World War II. Andrew Jackson's ignoring of the Supreme Court and Congress and Abraham Lincoln's use of near-dictatorial powers to prosecute the American Civil-War opened the door to the expansion of the authority and influence of the Executive branch and will be explored more a little later. The two Constitutional duties are as follows; the President must give regular reports on the "state of the union." This has become enshrined in tradition now, and the eponymously named "State of the Union Address" has become a major component of the American political circus. Interestingly, the Constitution does not specify how this 'regular report' ought to be given, and the first President merely wrote out a draft that was simply walked over by the Congress, where it was read without ceremony.

The second duty of the President as specified by the Constitution is to "take care that the laws of the nation are faithfully executed." This vague statement is largely responsible for the vast array of interpretations on the President's responsibilities of power and we will address some of them in the history section of this book. The Presidency today is a far different job than the one envisioned by the founders of the nation. The first and most common way the President implements their will, is through the use of Executive orders or signing statements.

An Executive order is a rule or order issued by the President to the Executive branch of the government and carries with it the force of law. The Executive branch, being the largest of the three branches of the U.S. government, wields tremendous power and is made up of fifteen departments. They are, in alphabetical order, Agriculture, Commerce, Defense, Education, Energy, Health and Human Services, Homeland Security, Housing and Urban Development, the Interior, Justice, Labor, State, Transportation, Treasury, and Veteran's Affairs Each of these is headed by a Presidential appointee called "The Secretary of Agriculture" and so on. The only exception is the head of the Justice Department who is called the "Attorney General."

Being able to delegate authority to cabinet offices and other governmental bodies, through Executive orders, is one of the President's key assets. A President issues Executive orders to help officers and agencies of the Executive branch operate on a day-to-day basis within the federal government itself. Orders have the full force of law if they deal with duties and powers directly given to the President by the Constitution or fall under the office's discretionary power. However, Executive orders only are in effect and apply to the administration that issues them. If an incoming President so chooses, they may rescind the Executive orders of a previous president.

Major policy initiatives enacted via Executive order still require approval by the legislative branch, especially when requiring money to implement but this does little to quell their power. Despite this, executive orders carry significant weight within the internal affairs of government. Among other things, Executive orders can decide how legislation will be enforced, or even if they will be enforced at all, as it is the Executive branch's responsibility to execute the laws of the land (it's all in the name…). Executive orders are also issued to deal with natural disasters and man-made emergencies, 72-hour military operations against hostile nations, and fine tuning the language of the broader legislation.

Remember how we mentioned that it's all in the name? As the head of the Executive branch, the President is constitutionally obligated to "take care that the laws be faithfully executed," as explained above. Tasked with this enormous responsibility, the Executive branch is by far the largest of the three, with over four million employees, including members of the military. Furthering their power, presidents can appoint thousands of Executive branch officials: an incoming president may make up to 6,000 before taking office and 8,000 more while serving. A particularly partisan President could use this power to fill these positions with ideologues and supporters, regardless of qualification. A President can also appoint a member of the opposing party to a post as a means of reconciliation after an election.

The most direct form of power the President can wield, "where the rubber meets the road" in international politics, is as Commander-in-Chief of the military. In this crucial and ever-increasing role, the President has seemingly unconstrained power. Congress can cut off funding to a military action but Representatives and Senators who are wary of the United States being seen as uncommitted to its responsibilities rarely threaten to do so. The Secretary of State, the country's head diplomat, answers directly to the President as well, so the President has the leading role in shaping America's missions abroad. While the power to declare war was given to the Congress by the Constitution, the President has ultimate responsibility for the military and sets its direction and missions.

Presidents have consistently initiated the process of preparing for and declaring war and then waiting for Congressional approval before the actual military operations start. We will learn later about how Presidents and Congress have expanded the power of the office of the President to authorize armed conflict or conduct military operations abroad. Critics have charged that numerous wars or large-scale invasions have happened even when presidents did not get official declarations from Congress, including, but in no way limited to prosecuting wars in the Philippines (1898), the Korean War (1950-53), the Vietnam War (1959-73), and the invasions of Grenada in 1983 and Panama in 1990. The President also serves as the de-facto leader of the party that they represent. The President appoints party leaders and sets its ideological direction. Their policies become the most important issues within the party, and the members work to further the President's agenda.

Chapter Two: Historical Presidents and How They Expanded the Office

Andrew Jackson was the first President to dramatically expand the power of the office. He did this through his popular mandate. Jackson was a wildly popular President, the first President that seemed to tap into a national mood. He advanced his agendas by forging direct links with the voters. He was the first President to routinely use colloquial language, powerful and plainspoken words that appealed to the common citizens. He was then, and remains today, quite controversial. His aggressive policies against the American Indians, using the power of the office, are blights on the Presidency and national history and have led to successful calls for his removal from the front of the twenty-dollar bill.

Further cementing his controversial legacy and expanding presidential authority, Jackson replaced many government officials on partisan grounds, inaugurating the "spoils system." Jackson fired cabinet members who wouldn't carry out his orders. This probably seems like a rational and reasonable course of action to today's readers, but in the America of the time, but it was scandalous in Jackon's day. In his eight years as President, Jackson went through four Secretaries of State and five Treasury Secretaries, both astonishing numbers of cabinet changes. By reversing the young nation's tradition of executive deference to Congressional power and by boldly casting himself as the people's Tribune he cast himself as their sole defender against special interests and their minions in the Congress. Jackson became the blueprint by which all "self-made" politicians would build their personal mythologies. In other ways, too, Jackson expanded the scope of presidential authority. He clashed with and distrusted his official cabinet appointees to such a great degree that Jackson devised and implemented his policies through a private group of friends and confidants that he termed the "Kitchen Cabinet." All subsequent presidents have relied on the Kitchen Cabinet to some degree, showing the power of connections, networking, and social circles among the powerful.

Abraham Lincoln also dramatically increased the power fo the office. This was partially due to necessity; the Civil War had literally torn the nation apart. It was also partially due to Congress being so bitterly divided that they were unable to pass any effective legislation. Lincoln's justifications, legal and moral or not, for disregarding the Constitution were rooted in the nation's existential crisis and his expansion of presidential power was a reflection of the traumas of his time. Lincoln suspended one of the foundations of the Western ideas of law and order, the necessity of *Habeas Corpus* (Latin for *"have the body"*), legal recourse through which people can challenge their unlawful incarcerations. Without *Habeas*

Corpus, people can be locked up at any time, for any reason, without suspicion or probable cause.

While Lincoln's greatness is undeniable, his decision to suspend one of the building blocks of American *jurisprudence* (standard laws and procedures) shows the dangers that unchecked power presents; even the best of men cannot resist abusing it. To paraphrase Lincoln, "If you want to test a man's character, give him power." We will cover shortly Woodrow Wilson and Franklin Roosevelt, both of whom committed gross violations of civil liberties as war-time Presidents out of perceived necessity. The Constitution is vague enough to allow for it to evolve and be manipulated in order to deal with issues of the day. It is in effect, a living document. However, some scholars, SCOTUS justices and other legal experts maintain the Constitution is static. The fight between the philosophies of a living document or a static one has been ongoing and central to the American legal system since 1789.Wilson imprisoned communists who dissented because of their political inclinations and Franklin Delano Roosevelt (commonly known as FDR) targeted the Japanese to be put into internment camps without just cause. He also expanded presidential power in other ways. Lincoln used his role as Commander-in-Chief to manage the army during the war, especially when his generals (especially George McClellan) were found to be lacking. President Lincoln's most enduring act, the drafting of the Emancipation Proclamation, was an expansion of Presidential power. Lincoln did this cleverly. His decision to end slavery was incremental; the legal precedent which allowed him to enforce the Emancipation Proclamation was the 13th Amendment, which abolished slavery and was only passed by Congress after the Confederate States surrendered.

Theodore Roosevelt's personal energy and boundless ambition were destined to clash with the limitations of the office. Teddy used something he called "the bully pulpit" to press his agenda. The bully pulpit was simply Roosevelt's term for the terrific platform the office of the President offered him to advocate for his agenda, both to the press and directly to the people. After the advent of mass media, all presidents became the bully at the pulpit. The enthusiastic and imperious Roosevelt informed the current role of the president in a military context as well. Roosevelt sent the Navy all over the world as a show of American might and superiority; while this was followed by a period of isolationism leading up to the two world wars, America's role as the world's policeman (for better or for worse) remains paramount to our national image and foreign policy.

Woodrow Wilson further expanded the Presidency during World War One through his power as Commander-in-Chief. In the wake of the war, his creation of the League of Nations cemented the United States as a world leader that would take the initiative in world affairs. This was a departure from American tradition dating back to George Washington's admonishment against getting involved in European alliances. It is difficult today to imagine the country as a an inward-looking isolationist power but that was the case when Wilson took office. His tenure as president changed that, for good or for ill, forever.

Wilson also changed the presidency domestically, as well. He was one of the first Presidents to take a profoundly active role in crafting and proposing legislation acting much like a Consul of the Roman Republic. You will find that ancient Roman laws, procedures, and imagery (like the two *Fascio* on either side of the Speaker of the House's seat in Congress) is very common in the American legal system and government. Wilson endeavored to work with, and often against the Congress to pass an agenda the President had crafted himself.

The Second World War brought about quite possibly the greatest expansion of power in presidential history. Franklin Delano Roosevelt was, in an odd parallel to the 2016 election, an obscenely wealthy New Yorker, who was famous primarily for his surname. He was elected four times, itself a huge expansion of the office. By the time WWII broke out in Europe, Roosevelt had been in power for half a dozen years already. He had been primarily concerned with the Great Depression. His "New Deal" was a program of legislation and Executive orders that changed the country's economic fortunes. Obviously, the use of Executive orders here is a great example of the expansion of presidential power or the use of power already granted the office through the actions of prior expansionist presidents like President Lincoln. Surely, disregarding the Constitution is the ultimate assertion of presidential power. Many historians and legal scholars maintain that the current power of the President makes him an "imperial president" in the realm of conducting armed conflict. While the President's legal authorities are still limited and checked domestically Congress has ceded their duty to authorize the use of arms to the office of the President.

Chapter Three: Electing the President

Alexander Hamilton laid out the philosophy for the Presidential election process and what would become the Electoral College in *The Federalist.*

"All these advantages will happily combine in the plan devised by the convention; which is, that the people of each State shall choose a number of persons as electors, equal to the number of senators and representatives of such State in the national government, who shall assemble within the State, and vote for some fit person as President. Their votes, thus given, are to be transmitted to the seat of the national government, and the person who may happen to have a majority of the whole number of votes will be the President. But as a majority of the votes might not always happen to center in one man, and as it might be unsafe to permit less than a majority to be conclusive, it is provided that, in such a contingency, the House of Representatives shall select out of the candidates who shall have the five highest number of votes, the man who in their opinion may be best qualified for the office."-*The Federalist Papers: No. 68-Alexander Hamilton 1788*

To put it in modern language, the people don't elect the president; they elect people to elect the president on their behalf. Contrary to the news speak, pundits, and a politician, the United States is not, nor ever was an Athenian democracy. It is a Federal Republic.

The founding fathers did this because they distrusted direct democracy and rarely resorted to it. The framers of the Constitution were not confident in the general public's ability to look after themselves and elect smart, reasonable, and responsible candidates. They were philosophical brethren of the Roman Senator, Lawyer, and former Consul Cicero. He once quipped; "There is no greater threat to our Republic than a moron with the right to vote." Because of this mistrust, they often instituted a measure of establishment control, having the public elect delegates and other representatives to do the political electing on their behalf.
The Electoral College is comprised of delegates from the States and these delegates elect the president. As they often were, the founders were vague and left it to the states to decide how those electors were chosen.

Forty-eight states use a winner take all method of appointing delegates. It doesn't matter how much a candidate wins the popular vote in a state, as long as you win, you get all the delegates. This is has been called undemocratic, and we'll learn about those criticisms of the system later. Two states award the delegates on a different basis, Maine and Nebraska. These two states are apportioned four electoral votes and have two Congressional districts each. In each state two electoral votes go to the statewide winner of the vote and the remaining two go to the winner(s) of the Congressional districts. These electors, the people that actually elect the president for the citizens of America, come from the dedicated party membership. Most of them are state party officials or volunteers rewarded for years of loyal service. Therefore, it is unlikely that they would vote for somebody other than who the party establishment has chosen.

On the first Tuesday (after the first Monday) in November voters will select a Presidential candidate on their ballots but they'll really be voting for electors who are expected to support that candidate. Several states list the electors under the candidates name but the system has existed for so long that it is usually taken for granted that a pledged elector will vote for their party's candidate.

There are currently 538 of these electors, and they make up the College. Why 538? The number of electors in each state is equal to the number of members of Congress to which the state is entitled, which is two senators and a proportional representation in the House based on the state's population. There are currently 435 members of the House and 100 Senators, and the Twenty-third Amendment granted the residents of Washington D.C while the same number of electors as the least populous state, currently three. This makes 538 members of the Electoral College. Because a majority of those 538 votes are needed to win the presidency, 270 is the magic number. It is possible, although unlikely given the dominance of the two-party systems in American politics that nobody could get to 270 votes. In this impractical scenario, the House of Representatives would select the president. Each State Delegation gets one vote, with the party with the most representatives in each state getting to decide the vote. If, somehow, the state delegation's vote is a tie, the state loses its votes, further disenfranchising voters. While this hot mess is going on, the Senate chooses the Vice President. Each senator gets one vote, with the relatively straightforward method of one vote per Senator. If, for some reason, the House cannot select a president, the vice president assumes the office.

The pros and cons of the Electoral College have long been debated. The merits and flaws of the system were most recently examined during the contested election of 2000, about which we will learn more in a little while. Opponents of the Electoral College cite examples of the elections in which the winner of the popular vote did not win the Electoral College and therefore lost the election. These critics think that having a leader elected who lost the popular vote violates some fundamental democratic principle and that the system should be abolished because it does not stick to the "one person, one vote" principle.

Swing States are at the center of our modern elections, and the media gives them constant coverage. Critics of the Electoral College system say it drives exclusive focus towards the larger swing states at the expense of the broader nation. According to these critics, the Electoral College encourages a campaign in which the candidates are forced to give all their attention to the few contested states. These critics argue that the candidate's time is better spent campaigning across the nation, in order to win a popular general election.

Furthermore, critics claim that the current system discourages voter participation. Aside from the few so-called "purple" states, states in which neither party is ideologically nor electorally dominant, voter turnout is largely insignificant due to entrenched political party affiliation. If you know your state is going to the Republicans or the Democrats, no matter how you vote, why bother spending the time going to the polls? Or so the criticism goes. On the other hand, if the presidential election were decided by a national popular vote, politicians, parties, and special interest groups would have a strong incentive to work to turn out the vote nationwide, as the general election would be the only votes that mattered. The swing states, where it is difficult to predict a winner, also receive a disproportionate amount of attention from the media and the candidates. This affects the policies they talk about and the agendas they present to the public, skewing the race even further.

The Electoral College has its defenders, also. Supporters of the current system argue that it forces candidates to build a popular base of support that is both geographically and ideologically diverse, due to having to appeal to the whole nation rather than just heavily populated urban areas. Proponents of the College fear that a simple popular vote would give disproportionate and damaging focus to the heavily populated Northeast and West Coast at the expense of the large swaths of the country that lives in more rural areas. In a "one person, one vote" system candidates might also be inclined to campaign hardest in their base areas to maximize turnout among core supporters, and ignore more closely divided parts of the country. Moreover, supporters of the current system say that it maintains the important federal nature and tradition of the United States.

The Electoral College also gives the states some freedom, while still binding them to a national system. Within Constitutional bounds, states are allowed to design their own laws on voting and enfranchisement (the right to vote), without undue influence from the federal level. A final bonus of the Electoral College, its supporters claim, is that it may help reduce the effects and isolate the instances of election fraud. Since the presidential election is not a nationwide general popular election, and electoral problems are confined to the state in which they happened. Also, the College helps prevent instances where a party dominant in one state, like the Republicans in South Carolina or the Democrats in New York, may dishonestly inflate the votes for a candidate and thereby affect the election outcome nationwide. An example of this isolation of fraud is that recounts can occur only on a state-by-state basis; imagine the impossibility of a national recount when we couldn't even get it right in Broward Country (but more on that later).

Twenty-six states have also taken on extra measures to ensure the electors vote for the candidate who receive the most statewide votes. These states "bind" their electors (much as some parties "bind" their delegates to a winning candidate) to the results of the statewide election. The other twenty-four states have no such laws to punish a so called "faithless elector." There have been very few cases of an elector voting for a candidate other than what the statewide vote should indicate and it has never happened in large enough quantities to change an election results. Check out information below to see if you'd be able to get your name printed under the wikipedia entry for "faithless electors" for your state.

States that bind their electors: Alabama, Alaska, Colorado, Connecticut, District of Columbia, Florida, Hawaii, Maine, Maryland, Massachusetts, Michigan, Mississippi, Montana, Nebraska, Nevada, New Mexico, North Carolina, Ohio, Oklahoma, Oregon, South Carolina, Tennessee, Utah, Vermont, Virginia, Washington, Wisconsin, Wyoming.

States that do not bind their electors: Arizona, Arkansas, Delaware, Georgia, Idaho, Illinois, Indiana, Iowa, Kansas, Kentucky, Louisiana, Minnesota, Missouri, New Hampshire, New Jersey, New York, North Dakota, Pennsylvania, Rhode Island, South Dakota, Texas, West Virginia.

The Electoral College leaves us with some interesting and essential footnotes. As we learned in 2000, when Al Gore won the popular vote but lost the Electoral College to George W. Bush, there is the possibility of an outcome that seems to contradict "the will of the nation." This has happened four times. We'll start at the beginning. In 1824, the election went to the House of Representatives. John Quincy Adams beat the aforementioned Andrew Jackson. An entire book, four times the length of this one, could be written on this complex and confusing election. It had a large number of candidates, none of whom had strong national support. Adams won in the New England states, Henry Clay won the West, and Jackson's support was scattered throughout the country. The future President Jackson received more electoral and popular votes than any other candidate, but failed to secure a majority. With no majority the election was thrown to the highly partisan House of Representatives which chose Adams to be president.
The election of 1876 was even closer; with Rutherford Hayes winning by only one electoral vote but somehow losing the popular vote by a stunning quarter of a million ballots. This was one of the most unbelievable results in American electoral history. In fact, it was so controversial that it is still in dispute today.

After the first count of votes, Tilden won 184 to Hayes's 165, with 20 votes still unresolved. These 20 electoral votes were in dispute in four states. Not shockingly, three were in the politically unstable South (the nation was still only a decade removed from the Civil War); Louisiana, South Carolina and, of course, Florida. Each party reported its candidate had won states still in dispute while one Oregon elector was declared illegitimate. Some observers predict that credentials challenges such as this will become an issue in 2016. The election was eventually given to Hayes by the narrowest of margins.

The election of 1888 was also complicated. Benjamin Harrison defeated Grover Cleveland. Harrison earned 233 electoral votes to Grover's 168 but, like all the others on this list, he lost the popular vote by 90,000. We learned about the importance of swing states earlier, and this election was focused on them. New York, New Jersey, Connecticut, and Harrison's home state of Indiana were all in play. Harrison and Cleveland split these four states, but a possibly fraudulent win in New York gave Harrison the election.

The most recent example of an election that did not go as planned was in 2000. George W. Bush didn't win the popular vote, losing by 540,000 but won the College by 271 to 266. The result of the election hinged on Florida, as it did in 1824, where the margin of victory was so close that it triggered a mandatory recount. Each party's lawyers repeatedly challenged the recounts but the Republican Secretary of State for Florida certified that the future President Bush had won. Nonetheless the outcome remained in doubt until the litigation finally reached the Supreme Court. The Court's decision in *Bush v. Gore* ended the recounts and effectively handed the election to Bush. The Florida vote was ultimately settled in favor of George W. Bush, by a margin of only 537 total votes, out of the six million cast in Florida and over one hundred million nationwide.

The Office of the Chief Executive of the United States (The President) is arguably the most powerful, stressful, and complex leadership position in the world. While presidential power has expanded in the realm of foreign affairs and military policy, their authority is still often constrained, stifled, and outright blocked for purely partisan reasons on a consistent basis. The President is not a King, nor a Shogun, and surely not a dictator. They are subject to the ever changing laws of the United States and must navigate the partisan rapids in Washington D.C to accomplish domestic policy agendas. Oddly enough, if the President wants to order military action against people on the other side of the planet, the President simply can and it is unlikely Congress would object. This power of the bullet is one that has come to define the office of the President since the Vietnam era. As we have discussed here, the American electoral process, despite claiming to represent the will of the people is often not Democratic at all. The process, the President, and the government, in general, are quasi-democratic; perhaps the ambiguous word "representative" is the most optimistic way to describe them. Regardless of which party in our two-party system, they all too often serve their corporate, business, and banking benefactors who "contribute' to their political campaigns. Americans may have the ability to choose between two candidates from two parties, but there are many other groups who have a say on which names even become a possibility to be on that ballot.

It is said that Ben Franklin was asked whether we were getting a Republic or a Monarchy. His response was "A Republic, if you can keep it." He knew that there would be groups who would try to take the business of governance as far away from the people as possible. His cynicism is still applicable today. Here we provided you an honest, unflinching look at presidential power and the process by which the most powerful person in the world is "elected" to office. We hope that you learned something that will affect how you digest politics and view our country.

List of Presidents of the United States

1. George Washington-Virginia

    Office: 1789-97   Party: Federalist

    Ancestry: English   Religion: Episcopalian (Protestant)

2. John Adams-Massachusetts

    Office: 1797-1801   Party: Federalist

    Ancestry: English   Religion: Unitarian (Protestant)

3. Thomas Jefferson-Virginia

    Office: 1801-09   Party: Democratic Republican

    Ancestry: Welsh   Religion: *No specific faith, likely an agnostic

4. James Madison-Virginia

    Office: 1809-17   Party: Democratic Republican

    Ancestry: English   Religion: Episcopalian (Protestant)

5. James Monroe-Virginia

    Office: 1817-25   Party: Democratic Republican

    Ancestry: Scottish   Religion: Episcopalian (Protestant)

6. John Quincy Adams-Massachusetts

    Office: 1825-29   Party: Democratic Republican

Ancestry: English   Religion: Unitarian (Protestant)

7. Andrew Jackson-Tennessee

    Office:1829-37   Party: Democrat

    Ancestry: Scots-Irish (Ulster Irish)Religion: Presbyterian (Protestant)

8. Martin VanBuren-New York

    Office: 1837-41   Party: Democrat

    Ancestry: Dutch   Religion: Dutch Reformed church (Protestant)

9. William Henry Harrison-Ohio

    Office: March-April 1841   Party: Whig

    Ancestry: English & Scottish   Religion: Episcopalian (Protestant)

10. John Tyler-Virginia

    Office: 1841-45   Party: Whig

    Ancestry: English   Religion: Episcopalian (Protestant)

11. James Polk-Tennessee

    Office: 1845-49   Party: Democrat

    Ancestry: Scots-Irish (Ulster Irish) Religion: Presbyterian (Protestant)

12. Zachary Taylor-Louisiana

    Office: 1849-50   Party: Whig

    Ancestry: English   Religion: Episcopalian

13. Millard Fillmore-New York

      Office: 1850-53   Party: Whig

      Ancestry: English   Religion: Unitarian

14. Franklin Peirce-New Hampshire

      Office: 1853-57   Party: Democrat

      Ancestry: English & Welsh   Religion: Episcopalian

15. James Buchanan-Pennsylvania

      Office: 1857-61   Party: Democrat

      Ancestry: Scots-Irish (Ulster Irish) Religion: Presbyterian

16. Abraham Lincoln-Illinois

      Office: 1861-65   Party: Republican

      Ancestry: English   Religion: *No specific faith

17. Andrew Johnson-Tennessee

      Office: 1865-69   Party: Democrat

      Ancestry: English & Ulster Irish   Religion: *No specific faith, likely agnostic

18. Hiram Ulysses Grant-Illinois

      Office: 1869-77   Party: Republican

      Ancestry: English & Scottish   Religion: Methodist (Protestant)

19. Rutherford Hayes-Ohio

      Office: 1877-81   Party: Republican

      Ancestry: Scottish   Religion: Methodist (Protestant)

20. James Garfield-Ohio

      Office: March-September 1881   Party: Republican

      Ancestry: English   Religion: Baptist (Protestant)

21. Chester Arthur-New York

      Office: 1881-85   Party: Republican

      Ancestry: Scots-Irish (Ulster Irish) Religion: Episcopalian (Protestant)

22. Grover Cleveland-New York

      Office: 1885-89   Party: Democrat

      Ancestry: English & Ulster Irish   Religion: Presbyterian (Protestant)

23. Benjamin Harrison-Indiana

      Office: 1889-93   Party: Republican

      Ancestry: English & Scottish   Religion: Presbyterian (Protestant)

24. Grover Cleveland-New York

      Office: 1893-97 *only President to serve two nonconsecutive terms

      Party: Democrat

25. William McKinley-Ohio

    Office: 1897-1901   Party: Republican

    Ancestry: Scots-Irish (Ulster Irish)   Religion: Methodist (Protestant)

26. Theodore Roosevelt-New York

    Office: 1901-09   Party: Republican

    Ancestry: Dutch & English   Religion: Dutch Reformed Church (Protestant)

27. William Howard Taft-Ohio

    Office: 1909-13   Party: Republican

    Ancestry: English   Religion: Unitarian (Protestant)

28. Woodrow Wilson-New Jersey

    Office: 1913-21   Party: Democrat

    Ancestry: Ulster Irish & Welsh   Religion: Presbyterian (Protestant)

29. Warren G. Harding-Ohio

    Office: 1921-23   Party: Republican

    Ancestry: English & Dutch   Religion: Baptist (Protestant)

30. Calvin Coolidge-Massachusetts

    Office: 1923-29   Party: Republican

    Ancestry: English   Religion: Congregationalist

31. Herbert Hoover-California

      Office: 1929-33   Party: Republican

      Ancestry: Swiss-German   Religion: Quaker

32. Franklin Delano Roosevelt-New York* only President to be elected to 4 terms

      Office: 1933-1945   Party: Democrat

      Ancestry: Dutch & English   Religion: Episcopalian (Protestant0

33. Harry S. Truman-Missouri

      Office: 1945-53   Party: Democrat

      Ancestry: English & Ulster Irish   Religion: Baptist (Protestant)

34. Dwight David Eisenhower-New York

      Office: 1953-61   Party: Republican

      Ancestry: Swiss-German   Religion: Presbyterian (Protestant)

35. John Fitzgerald Kennedy-Massachusetts

      Office: 1961-63   Party: Democrat

      Ancestry: Irish   Religion: Roman Catholic *first Catholic President

36. Lyndon Johnson-Texas

      Office: 1963-69   Party: Democrat

Ancestry: English & Ulster Irish   Religion: Baptist (Protestant)

37. Richard Millhouse Nixon-California

    Office: 1969-74   Party: Republican

    Ancestry: English   Religion: Quaker

38. Gerald Ford-Michigan

    Office 1974-77   Party: Republican

    Ancestry: English & Scottish   Religion: Episcopalian

39. James "Jimmy" Carter- Georgia

    Office: 1977-81   Party: Democrat

    Ancestry: English   Religion: Baptist

40. Ronald Reagan-California

    Office: 1981-89   Party: Republican

    Ancestry: Scots-Irish (Ulster Irish) Religion: Episcopalian

41. George H. W. Bush-Texas

    Office: 1989-1993   Party: Republican

    Ancestry: English   Religion: Episcopalian (Protestant)

42. William "Bill" J. Clinton-Arkansas

        Office: 1993-2001   Party: Democrat

        Ancestry: English & Ulster Irish   Religion: Baptist

43. George W. Bush-Texas

        Office: 2001-2009   Party: Republican

        Ancestry: English & Scottish   Religion: Evangelical Baptist (Protestant)

44. Barack H. Obama-Illinois* first President of African descent

        Office: 2009-2017   Party: Democrat

        Ancestry: Kenyan & Irish   Religion: Baptist

Recommended further reading

History in Quotations

The Constitution of the United States

www.fec.gov

The Quick and Dirty Guide to the Supreme Court of the United States

The Quick and Dirty Guide to the Electing and Understanding Congress

www.whitehouse.gov

www.congress.gov

Volume Three: The Quick & Dirty Guide to Electing and Understanding the United States Congress

Chapter One: Congress as Intended

The Congress of the United States of America is a bicameral legislative body formed under the US Constitution in 1789. It serves as one of three branches of government. Those three branches are as follows; Legislative (Congress), Judiciary (the courts), and Executive (the Presidency). In theory, all three branches have separate and balanced powers so that no one branch can subvert the will of the other two.

The founders of the United States wanted to prevent the Judiciary or Executive branch from becoming a tyrannical government. To that end, Article 1 of the Constitution established Congress and laid out the powers of that Congress, with an eye toward making that elected body the most important one. Article 1 seeks to keep the ability to legislate in the hands of the elected many; as opposed to the few or the one.

Article I of the Constitution sets forth the powers of Congress in a specific language. Section 8 states, "Congress shall have Power ... To make all Laws which shall be necessary and proper for carrying into Execution the foregoing Powers, and all other Powers vested by this Constitution in the Government of the United States, or in any Department or Officer thereof." Any senator or congressman may introduce a bill, after which it is referred to the appropriate legislative committee for hearings. The committee, in turn, debates the measure, possibly offering amendments, then voting on it. If approved, the bill heads back to the chamber from which it came, where the full body will vote on it. Assuming lawmakers approve the measure, it will be sent to the other chamber for a vote. The Congress also was given the sole responsibility to declare war, mint currency, allocate federal monies, control international trade, regulate all commerce, ratify treaties, form the armed forces, establish immigration rules, create federal courts, and impeach any federal official, elected or not.

The Tenth Amendment to the United States Constitution, which is part of the Bill of Rights, was ratified on December 15, 1791. The amendment supports the principle of federalism, which adheres to the outline of the original Constitution for the United States of America, by stating that the federal government is given only those powers assigned to it by the United States Constitution. All remaining powers are reserved for the states themselves. Congress proposed this amendment in 1789, following the Constitutional Convention. It was needed to meet the demands of the Anti-Federalism movement that opposed the creation of a strong central federal government. In short, this was implemented to secure states' rights. Moreover, the Congress is to practice something known as non-delegation. This is a principle in administrative law that states Congress cannot delegate its legislative powers to agencies. Instead, it instructs agencies to regulate, and must provide them an "intelligible principle" on which to base their regulations. This standard is viewed as quite lenient and has rarely ever been enacted to strike down legislation.

The authority with which Congress operates has both expanded in some respects and contracted in others. It rarely functions as intended by the founders of the country. One side of this coin regarding expansion of congressional power is their ability to regulate and investigate has expanded since the Great Depression; Congress now regulates all manner of goods, services, and general commerce. It can be argued that this falls under the Congressional duty to regulate trade and commerce. They have also expanded their authority in terms of investigation, and specifically into investigating and interfering with the private affairs of citizens. This can be seen in the cases of Terry Schiavo, the Major league Baseball steroid use scandal, and the Monica Lewinsky-President Clinton affair hearings. Congress now has the authority to investigate anything it can regulate under the authority of constitutional law. This expansion of congressional power in the investigative realm has been upheld by the US Supreme Court on several occasions.

The area in which the Congress had willingly ceded power to the Executive Branch is likely the most important duty Congress has: the right to declare war. The last time the US congress sat in full session to declare war with full constitutional legal authority was the US entry into the Second World War. Congress voted to declare war against the Axis Power of Imperial Japan on December 8th, 1941. Congress has since chosen to defer to the Presidency when it comes to armed conflicts. On dozens of occasions since the end of WWII Congress has given the President a nearly blank check to conduct undeclared war. They merely engage in an up or down vote to authorize force or do nothing at all, leaving the authorization of said the conflict in the hands of the Executive Branch.

Select sample list of military interventions involving the United States since WWII

1950-53 – The Korean War: The United States intervenes when North Korea invades South Korea. US forces deployed in Korea exceeded 300,000 during the last year of the active conflict (1953). Over 36,600 US military were killed in action. The conflict was backed by the United Nations and included the armed forces of the US, UK, Greece, South Korea, Australia, New Zealand, and West Germany. China would later enter the conflict on North Korea's side, thus forcing a stalemate which last to this day.

1959–75 – Vietnam War: American military advisers had been in South Vietnam since 1959, and their numbers had been increasing steadily as time went by. After referring to what he falsely termed were attacks on U.S. destroyers, President Johnson asked in August 1964 for a congressional authority expressing the U.S. goal to support "freedom and protect peace in Southeast Asia." Congress passed the Gulf of Tonkin Resolution, giving Johnson authorization for the use of conventional military force in Southeast Asia. Upon this action and following a Viet-Cong attack on an American base in central Vietnam, the United States escalated its participation in the war to a peak of 543,000 military personnel by April 1969.

1968-1970 – Laos & Cambodia: The United States starts secret bombing campaign against targets along the Ho Chi Minh trail in the sovereign nations of Cambodia and Laos. The bombings last at least two years.

1989–90 – Panama: United States invasion of Panama and Operation Just Cause, On December 21, 1989, President Bush revealed that he had ordered U.S. military forces to Panama to protect the lives of American citizens and bring General Noriega to justice. By February 13, 1990, all the American invasion forces had been withdrawn. About 200 Panamanian civilians were reported killed. The Panamanian President, General Manuel Noriega, was captured and brought to the U.S. to stand trial for an assortment of narcotics charges.

1991 – Iraq and Kuwait: The Gulf War. On January 16, 1991, in response to the refusal by Iraq to leave Kuwait after Iraq had swiftly invaded that small emirate, U.S. and Coalition aircraft attacked Iraqi forces and military targets in Iraq and Kuwait in conjunction with a coalition of allies and under United Nations Security Council resolutions. On February 24, 1991, U.S.-led United Nation (UN) forces launched a ground offensive that routed Iraqi forces and pushed them out of Kuwait within 100 hours. Military operations ended on February 28, 1991, when President Bush declared a ceasefire after utterly destroying Saddam Hussein's entire military

2001–2014 – Afghanistan: The War on Terror begins with Operation Enduring Freedom. On October 7, 2001, U.S. Armed Forces invade Afghanistan after the 9/11 attacks and begin combat action in Afghanistan against Al Qaeda terrorists and their Taliban supporters. The United States carries out anti-terror related activities in Georgia, Djibouti, Kenya, Ethiopia, Yemen, and the Philippines starting in 2004.

2003–2011 – Iraq: Operation Iraqi Freedom, March 20, 2003, The United States leads a coalition that includes the United Kingdom, South Korea, Australia, and Poland to invade Iraq with the public objective being "to disarm Iraq in pursuit of peace, stability, and security both in the Gulf region and in the United States."

Hussein and the Ba'athist Party are removed from power, the US and UK become an occupation force, and brutal sectarian civil war begins.

2014–present – Iraq & Syria: American aircraft bomb Islamic State positions in Syria. Airstrikes on Al-Qaeda, Al-Nusra Front and Khorasan positions are also being conducted. This also includes intervention against the Islamic State of Iraq and the Levant in Iraq as well.

There were also military actions in the following nations:

Lebanon	El Salvador
Colombia	Honduras
Eritrea	Nicaragua
Somalia	Ethiopia
Philippines	Libya
Sudan	Chad
Bolivia	The Congo (Zaire)
Haiti	Liberia
Dominican Republic	Central African Republic
Thailand	Sierra Leone
East Timor	Kenya
Bosnia	Mali
Macedonia	Angola
Kosovo	
Serbia	

*All military engagements and campaigns were conducted with cursory congressional approval or none whatsoever.

The War Powers Act is often mentioned in the media when the US engages in military conflict or operations such as drone strikes, air strikes, or Special Forces operations. It is the single law by which the Congress essentially gave up that body's Constitutional duty and authority to be the only branch of government to legally declare war. The law was passed in 1973, and it allows Congress to limit the President's use of military force. It was created in response to the unilateral war making powers that Lyndon Johnson and later Nixon exercised during the Vietnam War that went unchecked by the Congress. The War Powers act states that the President must tell Congress within 48 hours if he sends armed forces anywhere, and Congress must give approval for them to stay there for more than 90 days. While the language seems to limit the President's ability to launch military action it actually gives the President sweeping powers to conduct military operations whenever and where he sees fit. A recent example was US Special Forces, CIA operators, and logistical support being sent to Libyan rebels during their civil war against the Gaddafi regime. While President Obama was within his War Powers rights, he did not seek the congressional extension after the 90 days expired until the media began to speak about it. In this case, Congress still ceded their authority, even under the War Powers Act. They instead sighted the congressional "Use of Force" approval given in 2001 for the War on Terror as enough legal justification.

Chapter Two: The Structure of Congress

The House of Representatives

In the House of Representatives a congressman or congresswoman is elected to a two-year term. Article 1, Section 2 of the Constitution provides for both the minimum and maximum sizes for the House of Representatives. Currently there are five delegates representing the District of Columbia, the Virgin Islands, Guam, American Samoa, and the Commonwealth of the Northern Mariana Islands. A resident commissioner represents Puerto Rico. The delegates and resident commissioner hold the same powers as other members of the House, except that they may not vote when the House is meeting as the House of Representatives. In order to get elected, a representative must be at least 25 years old, a United States citizen for at least seven years and an inhabitant of the state he or she represents. Congressional districts are determined and redrawn every 10 years following the National Census. The election of a congressperson is altogether simple. In that, whichever candidate garners the majority of votes in a district wins. However, some states do require a bare minimum percentage to win. If no one candidate achieves this baseline percentage, a run-off election is held.

Among their duties, representatives introduce bills, resolutions, offer up amendments, and serve on committees. The number of representatives with full voting rights is 435, a number set by Public Law on August 8, 1911, and in effect since 1913. The number of representatives per state is proportionate to population.

The Senate

First convened in 1789, the composition and powers of the Senate are established in Article One of the U.S. Constitution. Every state is represented by two senators, regardless of population, who serve staggered six-year terms. Article I, Section 3 of the Constitution requires three qualifications for Senators. First, they must be at least 30 years of age. Second, they must have been citizens of the United States for the past nine years or longer, and third, they must be inhabitants of the states they seek to represent at the time of their election.

Elections to the Senate are held on the first Tuesday after the first Monday in November in even-numbered years, Election Day, is to coincide with elections for the House of Representatives. Senators are elected by their state as a whole. In most states (since 1970,) a primary election is held first for the Republican and Democratic parties, with the general election following a few months later. The winner is the candidate who receives a majority of the popular vote. In some states, runoffs are held if no candidate wins a clear majority.

The Senate has several exclusive powers not given to the House. These powers include; consenting to treaties as a precondition to their ratification and consenting to or confirming appointments of Cabinet secretaries, federal judges, other federal executive officials, military officers, regulatory officials, ambassadors, and other federal uniformed officers, as well as trial of federal officials impeached by the House. The Senate is widely considered both a more deliberative and more prestigious to be a member of than the House of Representatives. The Senate enjoys longer terms of office, smaller size, and state wide constituencies. The 17th Amendment allowed for citizens to actually elect their Federal Senators. Prior to the 17th Amendment, an ad-hoc system in each state was used to appoint their Federal Senator.

The Constitution allows several procedures and rules of order for the Senate that informs its ability to "check and balance" the powers of other areas of the Federal Government. Th Senate may advise and must consent to some of the president's government appointments. The Senate must consent to all treaties with foreign governments, try all impeachments, and it elects the vice president in the event no one gets a majority of the electoral votes.

The President can make certain appointments only with the advice and consent of the Senate. Offices whose appointments require the Senate's approval include members of the Cabinet, heads of most federal executive agencies, ambassadors, Justices of the Supreme Court, and other federal judges. Under Article II, Section 2 of the Constitution, a large number of government appointments are subject to potential confirmation; however, Congress has passed legislation to authorize the appointment of many officials without the Senate's consent. Normally, a nominee is first subjected to a hearing in front of a Senate committee that oversees that nominee's potential office. Following these hearings, which are public job interviews in essence, the nomination is considered by the full Senate. The legal authority of the Senate with regard to nominations is, however, subject to some constraints of the law. Take for example, the Constitution provides that the president may make an appointment during a congressional recess without the Senate's advice and consent. The recess appointment remains valid only temporarily; the office becomes open once again at the end of the next congressional session.

The Senate also is crucial in ratifying treaties. The Constitution states that the president may only "make Treaties, provided two-thirds of the Senators present concur." However, not all agreements with foreign powers are considered treaties under US domestic law, even if they are considered treaties under international law. Congress has passed legislation authorizing the president to make executive agreements without the input or consent of the Senate. In addition, the president may make congressional-executive agreements with the approval of a simple majority in each House of Congress, rather than a two-thirds majority in the Senate.

The Constitution requires the House of Representatives to impeach federal officials for "Treason, Bribery, or other high Crimes and Misdemeanors" and empowers the Senate to try these impeachments acting as the court in the matter. The House of Representatives has impeached sixteen officials, of whom seven were convicted. One official resigned before the Senate could complete the trial, thus making the legal proceedings moot. Only two presidents of the United States have ever been impeached: Andrew Johnson was impeached in 1868 and Bill Clinton in 1998. Both trials ended in acquittal; in the case of Andrew Johnson, the Senate came one vote short of the two-thirds majority required for a full conviction. Finally, under the Twelfth Amendment, the Senate also has the power to elect the vice president if no vice presidential candidate receives a majority of votes in the Electoral College during a general election.

Differentiated Constitutional powers of the House and Senate

The House of Representatives

Initiates all revenue bills (Art. I, Sec. 7)

Initiates (and passes or defeats) articles of impeachment (Art. I, Sec.2)

The Senate

The primary duty of the Senate is to give "advice and consent" on treaties (Art. II, Sec. 2) and to major presidential appointments (Art. II, Sec. 2).

Tries impeached officials (Art. I, Sec. 3).A premiere power enjoyed by the House is "the power of the purse." The Origination Clause, sometimes referred to as the Revenue Clause, is a key fiscal element of the United States Constitution. This clause states that all bills for raising money must start in the House of Representatives, but the Senate may propose or concur with amendments as in the case of other proposed bills.

While the Constitution provides authority to the House of Representatives to impeach an elected official, it appoints the Senate as the sole court for impeachment trials. The power of impeachment is limited to removal from office, but also allows for a removed officer to be disqualified from holding future public office. Fines and potential jail time for crimes committed while in office are left to the civil courts.

Congressional Committees

All proposed legislation lives or dies in a committee, whether they are passed into law or not. Hearings from interest groups and officials are held at the committee and subcommittee level. Committee members play vital roles in debates about the bills that are proposed. Moreover, committees help to organize and oil the most important machinery of Congress; that being considered, shaping, and passing laws to govern the nation. On average, 8,000 or so bills go to committee annually. Fewer than 10% of those bills make it out for consideration on the floor.

The Four Types of Committees

STANDING COMMITTEES: These powerful committees remain in force from one Congress to the next. They are the most important type because they consider and mold the vast majority of proposed laws. Standing committees can be fused together or discontinued, but most of them have been in session for decades. Standing committees also conduct investigations.

SELECT COMMITTEES: Select Committees are often temporarily formed for specific reasons, normally to dive into a particular issue of immediate importance. It is uncommon for them to actually draft legislation. Some, like the select committees to investigate the assassination of John F. Kennedy and the 9/11 Terrorist attacks, are intended to have limited duration. Others, like the Select Committee on Aging and the Select Committee on Indian Affairs, have existed for a number of years and do indeed produce laws. Sometimes long-standing select committees eventually become standing committees

JOINT COMMITTEE: This type of committee has similar purposes to that of select committees, however, they are made up of members from both the House and the Senate. They are set up to conduct business between the chambers and to help focus public attention on major issues. However, several joint committees handle routine matters, such as supervising national monuments.

CONFERENCE COMMITTEES: These are created only when the House and the Senate need to reach an accord over different versions of the same bill. A conference committee is made up of members from the House and Senate committees that initially debated the bill. Once the committee agrees on a compromise, the revised bill is returned to both houses of Congress for their study, and or approval.

Upon the conclusion of a congressional election cycle, political parties assign newly elected Representatives and Senators to various standing committees. They consider a member's own wishes in making the assignments, but they also look into the needs of the committees, in terms of region of the country, personalities, and party connections.

Since the House consists of 435 members, most Representatives only serve on one or two committees. Senators who have been in office for several election cycles very often serve on several committees and sub-committees at a time. Committee assignment is one of the most important choices for a new member's future work in Congress. Members seek appointments on committees that will facilitate their agendas for their districts or state. However, a member whose re-election is not in jeopardy and who has ambitions to be a leader in Congress, would want to be assigned to a powerful committee, such as Foreign Relations, Armed Services, or Ways and Means.

Standing Committees of Congress

HOUSE COMMITTEES	SENATE COMMITTEES
Agriculture	Agriculture, Nutrition, and Forestry
Appropriations	Appropriations
Armed Services	Armed Services
Banking and Financial Service	Banking, Housing, and Urban Affairs
Budget	Budget
Commerce	Commerce, Science, and Transportation
Education and the Workforce	Energy and Natural Resources
Government Reform	Environment and Public Works
House Administration	Finance

International Relations	Foreign Relations
Judiciary	Governmental Affairs
Resources	Health, Education, Labor, and Pensions
Rules	Indian Affairs
Science	Judiciary
Small Business	Rules and Administration
Standards of Official Conduct	Small Business
Transportation and Infrastructure	Veterans Affairs
Veterans Affairs	
Ways and Means	

The Chairperson of standing and special committees plays a leadership role in planning and coordinating the committee's work and in conducting its investigations. The Chair of a committee is responsible for acknowledging the members and witnesses who seek the floor to speak during sessions and for overseeing that any rules established by the committee be respected. In addition, the Chair is also responsible for maintaining order in the committee's proceedings, acting like a referee to some degree. However, the Chair does not have the power to censure or chastise disorder; this is solely the prevue of the House upon receiving a report from the committee pursuant to Standing Order 117.As the presiding officer of the committee, the Chair does not move on motions within the committee. The Chair also cannot vote, except in two situations: if there is a tie, in which case the Chair will cast the deciding vote. The second instance of a Chairperson voting is when a committee is considering a private bill. Whichever party has the majority in a given chamber, may pick who will be the chairman of a given committee.

Chapter Three: Corruption, thy name is Gerrymander

A political science dictionary will define the act of Gerrymandering as; "to manipulate the boundaries of an electoral constituency so as to favor one party or class or class over another." The term 'gerrymander' was initially written as Gerry-Mander, and is believed to have been used for the first time in the Boston Gazette on March 26, 1812. The word is an outgrowth and media reaction to the rearrangement of Massachusetts state senate election districts under Elbridge Gerry, who was the Governor of the state at the time. In 1812, Governor Gerry signed a bill that redistricted Massachusetts to the electoral benefit his Democratic-Republican Party. When seen on a map, one of the newly affected districts in the Boston area was likened to the shape of a salamander. The word Gerrymander itself came about as an amalgamation of the governor's surname and the word salamander. The redistricting was a brilliant success for the Democratic-Republicans in spite of the fact that the outcome of the 1812 election gave the Massachusetts House and governorship to the Federalists by a hefty percentage margin and cost Governor Gerry his job. The originally intended effect of a redistricted state senate was a success, with that legislative body remaining under Democratic-Republican majority. As for who coined the term Gerrymander, some historians point to Nathan Hale and the Russell brothers who were very vocal and widely read editors who supported the Federalists. However, there is no clear evidence linking these men to the word as its vernacular father.

Gerrymandering is used most often in favor of an incumbent elected office for the electoral benefits of a specific political party, always the one drawing the new map. Gerrymandering is particularly effective in non-proportional systems that have fewer parties, the fewer the better. A two party system is the most desirable field to engage in gerrymandering, allowing for more votes and voting districts to be apportioned to the party seeking the redistricting. Several countries like Canada, the UK, and Australia curb gerrymandering by authorizing non-partisan organizations to set constituency borders. Gerrymandering is most common in countries where elected politicians are responsible for defining constituency boundaries as part of their duties. The obvious self interest in the outcome of the process is clear, and the United States is a bright and shining example of this practice in full effect. In addition to its use achieving desired electoral results for a particular party, gerrymandering may be used to help or impede a specific demographic, such as a political, ethnic, racial, religious, or class group, such as in U.S. federal voting district boundaries that produce a majority of constituents representative of African-American or other minorities. The US national census, which is conducted once every ten years seems to be one of the primary demographic and statistical tools used when a party seeks to gerrymander a voting district. The principal goal of gerrymandering is voter suppression in favor of a party that generally performs poorly in a given district. There are several methods to accomplish this, they are as follows:

- "Cracking": This involves spreading voters of a particular type among many districts in order to deny them a sufficiently large voting bloc in any particular district.

- "Packing": The packing tactic aims to concentrate as many voters of one type into a single electoral district to reduce their influence in other districts.

- "Hijacking": Hijacking requires the redrawing of two districts in such a manner, that it forces two incumbents of the same political party to run against each other in one district, ensuring that one of them will be eliminated, thus leaving the other district to be won by someone from a different political party.

- "Kidnapping": This method aims to move areas where a specific elected official has significant support to another district, making it more difficult to win future elections with a new electorate. This is normally used against politicians who represent multiple urban areas. It removes larger cities from the district in order to make the district more rural and demographically amiable to a party with solid rural voter turn-out.

Chapter Four: Congressional Leadership Positions and Current leaders

<u>The House of Representatives</u>

Speaker of the House: Rep. Paul D. Ryan (Republican)

-The Speaker is elected by the entire House of Representatives. He serves as leader of the House and serves a number of roles. The Speaker's primary duty is being the presiding officer and administrative chief of the entire House of Representatives. In addition, the speaker serves as leader of the majority party in the House, and still maintains the representative role of an elected member of the House, although their party allegiance seldom is not on display. Finally, the Speaker of the House is 3rd in line to succeed the President, after the Vice President.

Majority Leader: Rep. Kevin McCarthy (Republican)

-The Majority leader represents the majority party on the House floor

Minority Leader: Rep. Nancy Pelosi (Democrat)

-The Minority leader represents the minority Party on the House floor

Majority Whip: Rep. Steve Scalise (Republican)

-The Whip acts to assist the party leadership in pursuing said party's legislative ambitions, "whipping up votes", or keeping Party members in line with the leadership's goals.

Minority Whip: Rep. Steny Hoyer (Democrat)

The Conference Chairman: Rep. Cathy McMorris Rodgers (Republican)

-This Chairman Helms organization of all Republican Party members in the House

Policy Committee Chairman: Rep. Luke Messer (Republican)

-They steer the party conference forum for policy creation and legal agenda development.

Assistant Democratic Leader: Rep. James Clyburn

-They most often work with the party caucuses and as liaison to Appropriations Committee.

Democratic Caucus Chairman: Rep. Xavier Becerra

-Commands the organization and direction of all Democratic Party members in the House.

The Senate

Vice President: Joseph Biden JR, (Democrat-Delaware)

-Second in line to the Presidency, and presides over the Senate. The VP only votes on legislation in cases of tie deadlocks.

Pro Tempore: Orin Hatch, (Republican-Utah)

- The president pro tempore of the Senate is to preside over the Senate in the absence of the Vice President.

Majority Leader: Mitch McConnell, (Republican-Kentucky)

Minority Leader: Harry Reid, (Democrat-Nevada)

Majority Whip: John Coryn, (Republican-Texas)

Minority Whip: Richard Durbin, (Democrat-Illinois)

Conference Chair: John Thune, (Republican-South Dakota)

Committee Chair: John Barrasso, (Republican-Wyoming)

Conference Vice-Chair: Roy Blunt, (Republican-Missouri)

Recommended further reading

The Constitution of the United States of America

History in Quotations

http://www.house.gov

http://www.senate.gov/index.htm

http://www.infoplease.com/ipa/A0931831.html

http://www.au.af.mil/au/awc/awcgate/crs/rl30172.htm

Volume Four: The Quick and Dirty Guide to the Supreme Court of the United States of America

Chapter One: Foundation, Intent, and Purpose

Like the other two branches of the US government, the Supreme Court has its origins in the Constitution. The Supreme Court is the highest court in the land and is the head of the Judicial branch of government. Article III, Section I, of the Constitution, provides that; "The judicial Power of the United States shall be vested in one Supreme Court, and such inferior Courts as the Congress may from time to time ordain and establish." The Supreme Court was created in accordance with this provision and by the legislative authority of the Judiciary Act of September 24, 1789. It was organized on February 2, 1790.

The ratification of the United States Constitution established the Supreme Court in 1789. Its powers are detailed in Article III of the Constitution. The Supreme Court is the only court specifically established by the Constitution, Congress created all the others. The Congress is also responsible for conferring the title "justice" to someone who sits on the Supreme Court. The Court first convened a session on February 2, 1790, by which time five of its six initial positions had been filled. The sixth member, James Iredell joined on May 12, 1790. At the time, the Court had only six members and every judgment that it made by a majority had to be by two-thirds. It should be noted that the Congress has always allowed the Court to make decisions with a partially full bench, starting with a set of four judges in 1789. Moreover, the Court was intended to be an apolitical and nonpartisan body. This has proven to be nearly impossible to see through. All Justices come to the Court with a certain set of political and philosophical stances. These positions often inform and influence the decisions of the Supreme Court but this "activist court" is rarely spoken of and almost never acknowledged by the Justices who sit on the Court.

The Supreme Court is commonly known as "SCOTUS." The court has final and largely discretionary appellate jurisdiction over all federal courts and state court cases involving issues of federal law. The Court also has original jurisdiction over a small range of cases. Moreover, the Supreme Court is the final interpreter of constitutional law on the federal level. However, it can only act within the context of a case in which it has jurisdiction. The Supreme Court has a special role to play in the United States system of government. The Constitution gives it the power to check the actions of the President and Congress. It can tell a President that his actions are not allowed by the Constitution and legally block any action by the President that the Court deems as being beyond the Constitutional powers of that office. The Court can also can rule that Congress passed legislation violating the Constitution and is no longer a law. It can also tell the government of a state that one of its laws breaks a rule in the Constitution.

The Supreme Court is not an all-powerful entity in the government. The Legislative and Executive branches limit its power. The principle of "checks and balances" is exercised even with respect to the Supreme Court. The President nominates justices to the court. The Senate must vote its approval of the nominations. The whole Congress also has great power over the lower courts in the federal system. District and appeals courts are created by acts of Congress. Unlike the Supreme Court, Congress can abolish lower courts if they so desire. The Supreme Court in essence, acts as a referee in a boxing match. The Congress, the President, the State Police, the Justice Department, the Department of Defense, and all other government officials and offices are the fighters in this analogy. Some can pass laws, and others can enforce laws. However, all exercise power within certain boundaries. These limitations are set forth by the Constitution. As the "referee" in the U.S. system of government, it is the Supreme Court's job to say when government officials step out-of-bounds and make rulings as to what is legal, and what is not. In simplified terms, interpretation of the intent of the Constitution is the primary function and power of the Supreme Court.

Over the past 200 plus years, the Court's powers have expanded beyond the original authority it possessed. This is a common theme throughout American history. All three branches of government have legislated and mandated legal powers to themselves that are well beyond the original intent spelled out in the Constitution. All political parties, all government officials, all three branches of government do this, despite denying the reality of it. On occasion, the Supreme Court makes rulings that expose and limit this practice. More often than not, however, the court ignores or endorses it. During the tenure of Chief Justices Jay, Rutledge, and Ellsworth from 1789–1801, the Court heard very few cases; its first decision was West v. Barnes in 1791, a case involving a procedural issue. The Court lacked a home of its own and had little prestige; a situation not helped by the highest-profile case of the era, Chisholm v. Georgia in 1793, involved a state's sovereignty and immunity from lawsuits. The judgment was reversed within two years from the adoption of the Eleventh Amendment.

The Court's power increased tenfold during the Marshall Court (1801–1835). Under Marshall, the Court established the power of judicial review over acts of Congress, including specifying itself as the supreme voice of the Constitution. Marbury v. Madison, arguably the most important case in Supreme Court history, was the first U.S. Supreme Court case to apply the principle of "judicial review". Judicial review is the power of federal courts to void acts of Congress in conflict with the Constitution. Written in 1803 by Chief Justice John Marshall, the decision played a key role in making the Supreme Court a separate branch of government on par with Congress and the Chief Executive (President). The Marshall Court also ended the practice of each justice issuing his opinion individually, a remnant of British tradition, and instead issuing a single majority opinion. Also during Marshall's tenure, although beyond the Court's control, the impeachment and acquittal of Justice Samuel Chase in 1804–1805 helped cement the principle of judicial independence. The Supreme Court, along with the Congress and the Executive Branch has spent every year since 1789 expanding its powers in order to keep up with the ever-expanding authority of the other two branches of government.

Chapter Two: Structure and Procedures of the Supreme Court

The current structure of the Supreme Court consists of nine justices. All justices who sit on the Court are nominated by a sitting President, and then are confirmed or rejected by the United States Senate. Since the Constitution does not dictate the size of the Court, it has grown over the centuries from its original composition of six justices. Article III of the United States Constitution leaves it to Congress to fix the number of justices. The Judiciary Act of 1789 called for the appointment of six justices. Congress later added justices to correspond with the growing number of judicial circuits: seven in 1807, nine in 1837, and ten in 1863.

In 1866, Congress passed a law demanding that the next three justices to retire would not be replaced, which would reduce the bench to seven justices. As a result, one seat was removed in 1866 and a second in 1867. In 1869, the Circuit Judges Act returned the number of justices to nine, where it has since remained without an increase in seats. Franklin D. Roosevelt attempted to enlarge the Court in 1937. His goal envisioned the appointment of one additional justice for each incumbent justice who reached the age of 70 years 6 months and refused retirement, up to a maximum bench of 15 justices. The proposal was claimed to be an attempt to ease the burden of the docket on elderly judges, but the actual purpose was widely understood as an effort to pack the Court with justices who would support Roosevelt's New Deal. The President's proposal to expand the Court failed in Congress. Despite FDR's failure to pack the Court, the balance shifted within six months when Justice Van Devanter retired and was replaced by Senator Hugo Black. By 1942, Roosevelt had appointed seven justices and elevated Harlan Fiske Stone to Chief Justice.

Associate Justices of the Supreme Court of the United States are the members of the Supreme Court. The number of Associate Justices is determined by the United States Congress and is currently set at eight by the Judiciary Act of 1869. Like the Chief Justice, Associate Justices are nominated by the President and are confirmed by the United States Senate by majority vote. This is provided for in Article II of the Constitution, which states that the President "shall nominate, and by and with the Advice and Consent of the Senate, shall appoint judges of the Supreme Court." Although the Constitution refers to them as "Judges of the Supreme Court," the title actually used is "Associate Justice," introduced by the Judiciary Act of 1789.

Article III of the Constitution specifies that Associate Justices and all other United States federal judges "shall hold their offices during good behavior." This language means that the appointments are effective for life, ending only when a Justice dies in office, retires, or is removed from office following impeachment by the House of Representatives and conviction by the Senate. The practice of lifetime appointments of judges to Federal courts has in recent years received much criticism.

Each of the Justices of the Supreme Court has a single vote in deciding the cases argued before it; the Chief Justice's vote counts no more than that of any other Justice. However, in drafting opinions, the Chief Justice enjoys additional influence in case disposition if in the majority through his power to assign who writes the opinion. Otherwise, the senior justice in the majority assigns the writing of a decision. Furthermore, the Chief Justice leads the discussion of the case among the justices. The Chief Justice has certain administrative responsibilities that the other Justices do not and is paid slightly more. The common salary is $255,500 per year for the Chief Justice and $244,400 per year for each Associate Justice. Associate Justices have seniority by order of appointment, although the Chief Justice is always considered to be the most senior. If two justices are appointed on the same day, the older is designated the senior Justice of the two. Currently, the senior Associate Justice is Anthony Kennedy. By tradition, when the Justices are in conference deliberating the outcome of cases before the Court, the justices state their views in order of seniority. If there is a knock at their conference room door, the junior justice, who sits closest to the door, must answer it. Under the law, when the Chief Justice is unable to conduct their functions or the office is vacant, the most senior Associate Justice carries out their duties.

The Court receives about 7,000 petitions every year. It has almost complete control over which cases it will hear. The justices choose about 90 percent of their 100 to 120 cases by writ of certiorari, an order to send up a case record from a lower court. Typically, the justices discuss any cases, one of them has recommended from earlier readings. The Rule of Four governs their choices: if four justices vote to hear a case, all nine agree to it. The court also tends to hear cases in which two lower courts have reached conflicting decisions. And it tends to look closely at lower court rulings that contradict earlier Supreme Court rulings.

The relationship between the Supreme Court and the other two branches of government is complicated. Depending on the political leanings of the Justices, and which party is in power in the Congress, or which party holds President's office, the Supreme Court can be friendly or adversarial. The Court is expressly supposed to a-political, but the reality is that the Court is highly partisan and ideological. Often, whichever party affiliation holds the majority in the Court makes judgments along that party's ideological lines.

Chapter Three: List of Justices & Landmark Decisions

LANDMARK CASES AND DECISIONS

Marbury V. Madison 1803

At the end of President John Adams' term, his Secretary of State failed to deliver documents commissioning William Marbury as Justice of the Peace in the District of Columbia. Once President Thomas Jefferson was sworn in, in order to keep members of the opposing political party from taking office, he told James Madison, his Secretary of State, to not deliver the documents to Marbury. Marbury then sued James Madison asking the Supreme Court to issue a writ requiring him to deliver the documents necessary to officially make Marbury Justice of the Peace. The Marbury v. Madison decision resulted in the establishment of the concept of judicial review. This allowed subsequent courts to review all laws passed by Congress and interpret their Constitutionality.

McCullough V. Maryland 1819

The U.S. government created the first national bank in the country in 1791, a time during which a national bank was controversial due to competition, corruption, and the perception that the federal government was becoming too powerful. Maryland attempted to close the Baltimore branch of the national bank by passing a law that forced all banks that were created outside of the state to pay a yearly tax. James McCulloch, a branch employee, refused to pay the tax. The State of Maryland sued McCulloch saying that Maryland had the power to tax any business in its state and that the Constitution does not give Congress the power to create a national bank. McCulloch was convicted and fined, but he appealed the decision. The Supreme Court determined that Congress has implied powers that allow it to create a national bank, even though the Constitution does not explicitly state that power, and that Maryland's taxing of its branches was unconstitutional.

Gibbons V. Ogden 1824

In 1808, the government of New York granted a steamboat company a monopoly to operate its boats on the state's waters, which included bodies of water that stretched between states. Aaron Ogden held a license under this monopoly to operate steamboats between New Jersey and New York. Thomas Gibbons, another steamboat operator, competed with Aaron Ogden on this same route but held a federal coasting license issued by an act of Congress. Ogden filed a complaint in New York court to stop Gibbons from operating his boats, claiming that the monopoly granted by New York was legal even though he operated on shared, interstate waters. Gibbons disagreed arguing that the U.S. Constitution gave Congress the sole power over interstate commerce. After losing twice in New York courts, Gibbons appealed the case to the Supreme Court. The Supreme Court determined that the Commerce clause of the Constitution grants the federal government the power to determine how interstate commerce is conducted.

Dred Scott V. Sanford 1857

In 1834, slave Dred Scott was purchased in Missouri and then brought to Illinois, a free (non-slave) state. He and his owner later moved to present-day Minnesota where slavery had been recently prohibited, and then back to Missouri. When his owner died, Scott sued the widow to whom he was left, claiming he was no longer a slave because he had become free after living in a free state. At a time when the country was in deep conflict over slavery, the Supreme Court decided that Dred Scott was not a "citizen of the state", so they had no jurisdiction in the matter, but the majority opinion also stated that he was not a free man.

Plessy V. Ferguson 1896

In 1890, Louisiana passed a statute called the Separate Car Act declaring that all rail companies carrying passengers in Louisiana must provide separate but equal accommodations for white and non-white passengers. The penalty for sitting in the wrong compartment was a fine of $25 or 20 days in jail. A group of black citizens joined forces with the East Louisiana Railroad Company to fight the Act. In 1892, Homer Plessy, who was one-eighth black, purchased a first-class ticket and sat in the white-designated railroad car. Plessy was arrested for violating the Separate Car Act and argued in court that the Act violated the Thirteenth and Fourteenth Amendments to the Constitution. After losing twice in the lower courts, Plessy took his case to the U.S. Supreme Court, which upheld the previous decisions that racial segregation is constitutional under the separate but equal doctrine.

Korematsu V. The United States 1944

After Pearl Harbor was bombed in December 1941, the military feared a Japanese attack on the U.S. mainland and the American government was worried that Americans of Japanese descent might aid the enemy. In 1942, President

Franklin D. Roosevelt signed an executive order forcing many West Coast Japanese and Japanese Americans into internment camps. Fred Korematsu, a Japanese American, relocated and claimed to be Mexican-American to avoid being interned, but was later arrested and convicted of violating an executive order. Korematsu challenged his conviction in the courts saying that Congress, the President, and the military authorities did not have the power to issue the relocation orders and that he was being discriminated against based on his race. The government argued that the evacuation was necessary to protect the country, and the federal appeals court agreed. Korematsu appealed this decision and the case came before the U.S. Supreme Court. The Court agreed with the government and stated that the need to protect the country was a greater priority than the individual rights of the Japanese and Japanese Americans. Essentially the Court adopted the old Roman axiom of; "Inter arma enim silent leges", in war the law is silent.

Brown V. Kansas Board of Education 1954

In Topeka, Kansas in the 1950s, schools were segregated by race. Each day, Linda Brown and her sister had to walk through a dangerous railroad switchyard to get to the bus stop for the ride to their all-black elementary school. There was a school closer to the Brown's house, but it was only for white students. Linda Brown and her family believed that the segregated school system violated the Fourteenth Amendment and took their case to court. Federal district court decided that segregation in public education was harmful to black children, but because all-black schools and all-white schools had similar buildings, transportation, curricula, and teachers, the segregation was legal. The Browns appealed their case to Supreme Court stating that even if the facilities were similar, segregated schools could never be equal to one another. The Court decided that state laws requiring separate but equal schools violated the Equal Protection Clause of the Fourteenth Amendment.

Mapp V. Ohio 1961

Suspicious that Dollree Mapp might be hiding a person suspected in a bombing, the police went to her home in Cleveland, Ohio. They knocked on her door and demanded entrance, but Mapp refused to let them in because they did not have a warrant. After observing her house for several hours, the police forced their way into Mapp's house and held up a piece of paper when Mapp demanded to see their search warrant. As a result of their search, the police found a trunk containing pornographic materials. They arrested Mapp and charged her with violating an Ohio law against the possession of obscene materials. At the trial, the police officers did not show Mapp and her attorney the alleged search warrant or explain why they refused to do so. Nevertheless, the court found Mapp guilty and sentenced her to jail. After losing an appeal to the Ohio Supreme Court, Mapp took her case to the U.S. Supreme Court. The Court determined that evidence obtained through a search that violates the Fourth Amendment is inadmissible in state courts.

Gideon V. Wainwright 1963

In June 1961, a burglary occurred at the Bay Harbor Pool Room in Panama City, FL. Police arrested Clarence Earl Gideon after he was found nearby with a pint of wine and some change in his pockets. Gideon, who could not afford a lawyer, asked a Florida Circuit Court judge to appoint one for him arguing that the Sixth Amendment entitles everyone to a lawyer. The judge denied his request and Gideon was left to represent himself. He did a poor job of defending himself and was found guilty of breaking and entering and petty larceny. While serving his sentence in a Florida state prison, Gideon began studying law, which reaffirmed his belief that his rights were violated when the Florida Circuit Court refused his request for counsel. From his prison cell, he hand wrote a petition asking the U.S. Supreme Court to hear his case, and it agreed. The Court unanimously ruled in Gideon's favor, stating that the Sixth Amendment requires state courts to provide attorneys for criminal defendants who cannot otherwise afford counsel.

Miranda V. Arizona 1966

Ernesto Miranda was arrested after a crime victim identified him, but police officers questioning him did not inform him of his Fifth Amendment right against self-incrimination, or of his Sixth Amendment right to the assistance of an attorney. While he confessed to the crime, his attorney later argued that his confession should have been excluded from the trial. The Supreme Court agreed, deciding that the police had not taken proper steps to inform Miranda of his rights.

Tinker V. Des Moines School District 1969

John and Mary Beth Tinker of Des Moines, Iowa, wore black armbands to their public school as a symbol of protest against American involvement in the Vietnam War. When school authorities asked that the Tinkers remove their armbands, they refused and were subsequently suspended. The Supreme Court decided that the Tinkers had the right to wear the armbands, with Justice Abe Fortas stating that no one expects students to "shed their constitutional rights to freedom of speech or expression at the schoolhouse gate."

Roe V. Wade 1973

Jane Roe was an unmarried and pregnant Texas resident in 1970. Texas law made it a felony to abort a fetus unless "on medical advice for the purpose of saving the life of the mother." Roe filed suit against Wade, the district attorney of Dallas County, contesting the statue on the grounds that it violated the guarantee of personal liberty and the right to privacy implicitly guaranteed in the First, Fourth, Fifth, Ninth, and Fourteenth Amendments. In deciding for Roe, the Supreme Court invalidated any state laws that prohibited first trimester abortions.

United States V. Richard M. Nixon 1974

A congressional hearing about President Nixon's Watergate break-in scandal revealed that he had installed a tape-recording device in the Oval Office. The special prosecutor in charge of the case wanted access to these taped discussions to help prove that President Nixon and his aides had abused their power and broken the law. President Nixon's incomplete compliance with the special prosecutor's demands was challenged and eventually taken to the Supreme Court of the United States. The Court decided that executive privilege is not limitless, and the tapes were released.

University of California V. Bakke 1978

In the early 1970s, the medical school of the University of California at Davis devised a dual admissions program to increase representation of disadvantaged minority students. Allan Bakke was a white male who applied to and was rejected from the regular admissions program, while minority applicants with lower grade point averages and testing scores were admitted under the specialty admissions program. Bakke filed suit, alleging that this admissions system violated the Equal Protection Clause and excluded him on the basis of race. The Supreme Court found for Bakke against the rigid use of racial quotas, but also established that race was a permissible criterion among several others.

New Jersey V. T.L.O 1985

A New Jersey high school student was accused of violating school rules by smoking in the bathroom, leading an assistant principal to search her purse for cigarettes. The Vice Principal discovered marijuana and other items that implicated the student in dealing marijuana. The student tried to have the evidence from her purse suppressed, contending that mere possession of cigarettes was not a violation of school rules; therefore, a desire for evidence of smoking in the restroom did not justify the search. The Supreme Court decided that the search did not violate the Constitution and established more lenient standards for reasonableness in school searches. This has opened the door for abuse of power by law enforcement in that they now do not strictly need a warrant to search your person, or property. They need only "prove" reasonable suspicion.

Hazelwood V. Kuhlmeier 1988

Hazelwood East High School Principal Robert Reynolds procedurally reviewed the Spectrum, the school's student-written newspaper, before publication. In May 1983, he decided to have certain pages pulled because of the sensitive content in two of the articles, and acted quickly to remove them in order to meet the paper's publication deadline. The journalism students felt that this censorship was a direct violation of their First Amendment rights. The Supreme Court decided that Principal Reynolds had the right to such editorial decisions, as he had "legitimate pedagogical concerns." However, it should be noted that the Court has previously ruled the KKK was allowed to protest and spew violent rhetoric. It seems that the age of the person involved can limit one's rights as a citizen.

Texas v. Johnson 1989

In 1984 Gregory Lee Johnson was arrested in Dallas for burning the American flag. He was convicted of violating a Texas law that made it a crime to intentionally desecrate a state or national flag. Texas was not alone in this as 47 other states also prohibited this type of demonstration. Justice Brennan wrote for a 5-to-4 majority "Government may not prohibit the expression of an idea because society finds the idea itself offensive or disagreeable."

Cruzan v. Missouri Dept. of Health 1990

While the Constitution protects a person's right to reject life-preserving medical treatment (their "right to die"), states can regulate that interest if the regulation is reasonable. Nancy Cruzan lay in a permanent vegetative state as a result of injuries suffered in an auto accident. Her parents sought to withdraw life-sustaining treatment and allow her to die; claiming she'd said this would be her wish under such circumstances. The state refused, and the Supreme Court upheld the state's guidelines for the continuation of medical treatment, which allowed withdrawal of treatment only with clear and convincing evidence that this is what the patient would have wanted. The Court said that, given the need to protect against abuses of such situations, the state could continue life support as long as its standards for doing so are reasonable.

Citizens United V. Federal Election Commission 2010

Citizens United sought an injunction against the Federal Election Commission in the United States District Court for the District of Columbia to prevent the application of the Bipartisan Campaign Reform Act (BCRA) to its film Hillary: The Movie. The Movie expressed opinions about whether Senator Hillary Rodham Clinton would make a good President. In an attempt to regulate "big money" campaign contributions, the BCRA applies a variety of restrictions to "electioneering communications." Section 203 of the BCRA prevents corporations or labor unions from funding such communication from their general treasuries. Sections 201 and 311 require the disclosure of donors to such communication and a disclaimer when the candidate it intends to support does not authorize the communication. Citizens United argued that: 1) Section 203 violates the First Amendment on its face and when applied to The Movie and its related advertisements, and that 2) Sections 201 and 203 are also unconstitutional as applied to the circumstances.

The United States District Court denied the injunction. Section 203 on its face was not unconstitutional because the Supreme Court in McConnell v. FEC had already reached that determination. The District Court also held that The Movie was the functional equivalent of express advocacy, as it attempted to inform voters that Senator Clinton was unfit for office, and thus Section 203 was not unconstitutionally applied. Lastly, it held that Sections 201 and 203 were not unconstitutional as applied to The Movie or its advertisements. The court reasoned that the McConnell decision recognized that disclosure of donors "might be unconstitutional if it imposed an unconstitutional burden on the freedom to associate in support of a particular cause," but those circumstances did not exist in Citizen United's claim.

Ultimately this ruling allows any person, or group to contribute massive amounts of money to a candidate's election campaign. In addition, it says that the candidate is not obliged to report how much or from whom the money came. This decision allows for foreign countries, businesses, and other interests to "buy' American elected officials through campaign contributions. The potential for abuse is clear but a recourse that will fully protect the first amendment without the campaign finance excesses Citizens United has allowed has yet to fleshed out.

Obergefell v. Hodges 2015

This important Supreme Court case upheld the fundamental right to marry is guaranteed to same-sex couples by both the Due Process Clause and the Equal Protection Clause of the Fourteenth Amendment to the United States Constitution. In November 2014, following an arduous series of appeals court rulings from the Fourth, Seventh, Ninth, and Tenth Circuits that state-level bans on same-sex marriage were unconstitutional, the Sixth Circuit ruled that it was bound by Baker v. Nelson and found such bans are constitutional. This created a split between circuits and led to a nearly mandatory Supreme Court review of the case. The SCOTUS decision came down on June 26, 2015. Obergefell overturned Baker and requires all states to issue marriage licenses to same-sex couples and to recognize same-sex marriages validly performed in other jurisdictions. The judgment legalized same-sex marriage throughout the United States, its possessions, and her territories. Due to their legal status being ambiguous at best, the status of same-sex marriage in American Samoa remains uncertain. Some states are still taking steps to try and deny same-sex marriage under a series of state laws and mandates that seek to circumvent the Supreme Court and institutionalize the perceived homophobia of the residents. There is every possibility that this case will spawn others that will have to be adjudicated by the Court.

Justices of the Supreme Court of the United States

John Jay	**New York**	**1789-95**
Jonathan Rutledge	South Carolina	1789-91
William Cushing	Massachusetts	1789-1810
James Wilson	Pennsylvania	1789-98
John Blair Jr.	Virginia	1789-95
James Iredell	North Carolina	1790-99
Thomas Johnson	Maryland	1792-93
William Paterson	New Jersey	1793-1806
John Rutledge	**South Carolina**	**1795 * second term after resigning**
Samuel Chase	Maryland	1796-1811
Oliver Ellsworth	**Connecticut**	**1796-1800**
Bushrod Washington	Virginia	1798-1829
Alfred Moore	North Carolina	1800-04
John Marshall	**Virginia**	**1801-35**
William Johnson	South Carolina	1804-34
Henry H. Livingston	New York	1807-23
Thomas Todd	Kentucky	1807-26
Gabriel Duvall	Maryland	1811-35
Joseph Story	Massachusetts	1812-45
Smith Thompson	New York	1823-43
Robert Trimble	Kentucky	1826-28
John McLean	Ohio	1829-61

Henry Baldwin	Pennsylvania	1830-44
James M. Wayne	Georgia	1835-67
Roger Taney	**Maryland**	**1836-64**
Philip Barbour	Virginia	1836-41
John Carton	Tennessee	1837-65
John McKinley	Alabama	1837-52
Peter Daniel	Virginia	1842-60
Samuel Nelson	New York	1845-72
Levi Woodbury	New Hampshire	1845-51
Robert C. Grier	Pennsylvania	1846-70
Benjamin Curtis	Massachusetts	1851-57
John Campbell	Alabama	1853-61
Nathan Clifford	Maine	1858-81
Noah Swayne	Ohio	1862-81
Samuel Miller	Iowa	1862-90
David Davis	Illinois	1862-77
Stephen Field	California	1863-97
Salmon Chase	**Ohio**	**1864-73**
William Strong	Pennsylvania	1870-80
Joseph Bradley	New Jersey	1870-92
Ward Hunt	New York	1873-82
Morrison Waite	**Ohio**	**1874-88**
John Harlan	Kentucky	1877-1911
William Woods	Alabama	1881-87

Stanley Matthews	Ohio	1881-89
Horace Gray	Massachusetts	1882-1902
Samuel Blatchford	New York	1882-93
Lucius Lamar	Mississippi	1888-93
Melville Fuller	**Illinois**	**1888-1910**
Davis Brewer	Kansas	1890-1910
Henry Brown	Michigan	1891-1906
George Shiras Jr.	Pennsylvania	1892-1903
Howell Jackson	Tennessee	1893-95
Edward White	**Louisiana**	**1894-1921**
Rufus Peckham	New York	1896-1909
Joseph McKenna	California	1898-1925
Oliver Holmes Jr.	Massachusetts	1902-32
William R. Day	Ohio	1903-22
William Moody	Massachusetts	1906-10
Horace Lurton	Tennessee	1910-14
Charles Hughes	New York	1910-16
Willis Devanter	Wyoming	1911-37
Joseph Lamar	Georgia	1911-16
Mahlon Pitney	New Jersey	1912-22
James McReynolds	Tennessee	1914-41
Louis Brandeis	Massachusetts	1916-39
John Hessin Clarke	Ohio	1916-22
William H. Taft	**Ohio**	**1921-30 *only former President on SCOTUS**

George Sutherland	Utah	1922-38
Pierce Butler	Minnesota	1923-39
Edward Sanford	Tennessee	1923-30
Harlan Stone	New York	1925-46
Charles Hughes	**New York**	**1930-41*second term on the Court**
Owens Roberts	Pennsylvania	1930-45
Benjamin Cardozo	New York	1932-38*first Catholic on the Court
Hugo Black	Alabama	1937-71
Stanley Reed	Kentucky	1938-57
Felix Frankfurter	Massachusetts	1939-62
William Douglas	Connecticut	1939-75
Frank Murphy	Michigan	1940-49
Harlan F. Stone	**New York**	**1941-46**
James Byrnes	South Carolina	1941-42
Robert Jackson	New York	1941-54
Wiley Rutledge	Iowa	1943-49
Harold Burton	Ohio	1945-58
Fred Vinson	**Kentucky**	**1946-53**
Tom Clark	Texas	1949-67
Sherman Minton	Indiana	1949-56
Earl Warren	**California**	**1953-69**
John Harlan II	New York	1955-71
William Brennan	New Jersey	1956-90
Charles Whitaker	Missouri	1957-62

Potter Stewart	Ohio	1958-81
Bryon White	Colorado	1962-93
Arthur Goldberg	Illinois	1962-65* first person of Jewish heritage on the court
Abe Fortas	Tennessee	1965-69
Thurgood Marshall	New York	1967-91*first African-American on the Court
Warren Burger	**Minnesota**	**1969-86**
Harry Blackmun	Minnesota	1970-94
Lewis Powell Jr.	Virginia	1972-87
William Rehnquist	**Arizona**	**1972-2005**
John Paul Stevens	Illinois	1975-2010
Sandra O'Connor	Arizona	1981-2006*first woman on the court
Antonin Scalia	Virginia	1986-2016
Anthony Kennedy	California	1988-Present
David Souter	New Hampshire	1990-2009
Clarence Thomas	Georgia	1991-Present
Ruth Bader Ginsburg	Washington DC	1993-Present
Stephen Breyer	Massachusets	1994-Present
John G. Roberts	Maryland	2005-Present
Samuel Alito	New Jersey	2006-Present
Sonia Sotomayor	New York	2009-Present* First Hispanic on court
Elena Kagan	Massachusets	2010-Present

-

Chapter Four: How the Court works in reality & Criticisms of SCOTUS

Despite the Constitution stating that the Supreme Court is to be nonpartisan and apolitical, the fact of the matter is that the Court is extremely political. Depending on which party enjoys the majority of seats on the Court, one can see how decisions come down along party lines. Currently, the conservatives hold sway on the Court, with five of nine Justices being registered Republicans and clearly leaning to that end of the spectrum when arguing and deciding cases. When a President chooses a person to sit on the court, and they are confirmed, this allows that President's party to have influence, and at times, dominate the Supreme Court. While there had been instances of Justices voting outside their party's ideology, such as recently when Chief Justice Roberts voted in favor of gay marriage, this is a rare occurrence.

Often in the media one will hear the various talking heads and elected officials accuse the Court of being an "activist court." This term refers to the Court making judgments based on their political ideology. The Justices normally deny their individual "activism", however, from the voting records and judgments made, "activism" within the Supreme cannot be denied.

Perhaps no event better illustrates the power of the United States Supreme Court than the results of the 2000 presidential general election. Just when you thought the separation of powers issue had been settled once and for all, the Court stepped in to adjudicate who had won the biggest political contest of all. Legions of Court watchers, law professors, media commentators, and armchair legal analysts across the country thought the Court's willingness to step into the fray was a major seizure of power and a gross corruption of the law. Others were grateful that the electoral crisis was being brought to a close.

Election night 2000 was a cliffhanger that went on for weeks. Many people went to bed that night thinking that Al Gore had won, only to discover in the morning that George W. Bush had been declared the winner. In fact, the election was simply too close to call. Several states were up for grabs, but in the end, it came down to one: Florida, where Bush's younger brother, Jeb, was governor. Florida electors were unable to commit themselves to either Bush or Gore owing to the closeness of the vote. Brush fires erupted in several precincts where the candidates' surrogates traded allegations about various improprieties. Recounts were started, then stopped as Republicans and Democrats wrangled over what standards to apply. It was more than a little chaotic.

The Supreme Court actually imposed itself into the election on three occasions. Only the last two are known as Bush v. Gore. In the first of these cases, Bush v.

Palm Beach County Canvassing Board, the Court hoped to end the election crisis by putting a stop to the Florida Supreme Court's decision to extend the time for certifying the vote past the period set by state law. But by the time the Court began hearing arguments in the appeal on December 1, the certification had already occurred. The justices returned the case back to the Florida Supreme Court, instructing the lower court to rewrite its opinion so that it would not create a conflict between state and federal law. A week later, the Florida Supreme Court demanded a statewide recount of ballots. Unlike its earlier decision, this one was not unanimous.

When the Florida justices were split 4-3, the U.S. Supreme Court once again exercised its appellate review jurisdiction and granted "certiorari', Latin for review, to Bush v. Gore. The day after the Florida Supreme Court had ordered a recount, the U.S. Supreme Court granted a temporary delay (stay) in enforcing the Florida Supreme Court's order. The U.S. Supreme Court justices, too, were narrowly divided, 5-4. The five justices voting in favor of the stay were the same five conservatives who had been moving the Rehnquist Court to the right for more than a decade. Not to mention several had been appointed to the Court via President Reagan or President George H.W. Bush. The first hearing of Bush v. Gore expressed to the nation what would happen if the Court took further action in the case. The Court's third and final intervention in the 2000 presidential election came several days later. In its unsigned opinion, the Court explained that it had voted 5-4 to put a stop to the Florida recount. Allowing the recount to go forward, the Court said, "would violate the Equal Protection Clause of the Fourteenth Amendment." The U.S. Supreme Court sent the case back down to the Florida Supreme Court, which had no alternative but to dismiss it. The presidential election of 2000 had been decided, in essence, by the vote of one Supreme Court justice. The Constitution states that the Congress is to decide such things, but the Congress said nothing, asserted no power in the case, and allowed the Supreme Court to expand its authority tremendously. The Twelfth Amendment stipulates that in a contested presidential election, "The President of the Senate shall, in the presence of the Senate and the House of Representatives, open all the certificates and the votes shall then be counted."

The Court's judgment breaks down as follows:

1.) Seven justices (the five-Justice majority plus Breyer and Souter) agreed that there was an Equal Protection Clause violation in using different standards of counting in different counties.

2.) Five justices agreed that December 12 (the date of the decision) was the deadline Florida had established for recounts. Kennedy, O'Connor, Rehnquist,

Scalia and Thomas in support; Breyer, Ginsburg, Souter and Stevens opposed. Justices Breyer and Souter wanted to remand the case to the Florida Supreme Court to permit that court to establish uniform standards of what constituted a legal vote and then conduct a hand recount all ballots using those standards.

3.) Three justices (Rehnquist, Scalia and Thomas) argued that the Florida Supreme Court had acted contrary to the intent of the Florida legislature. Four justices (Breyer, Souter, Ginsburg, and Stevens) specifically disputed this in their dissenting opinions, and the remaining two Justices (Kennedy and O'Connor) declined to join Rehnquist's position on the matter.

The decision allowed Florida Secretary of State Katherine Harris's previous certification of George W. Bush as the winner of Florida's 25 electoral votes to stand. Florida's votes gave Bush, the Republican candidate, 271 electoral votes, and one more than the required 270 electoral votes to win the Electoral College and defeat Democratic candidate Al Gore, who received 266 electoral votes. Media organizations subsequently analyzed the ballots, and under the strategy that Al Gore employed at the beginning of the Florida recount, filing a lawsuit to force hand recounts in four predominantly Democratic counties, Bush would have kept his lead regardless. On the other hand, an independent nonpartisan study also found that a state wide tally would have revealed Al Gore as the victor by 60 to 171 votes, if the official vote-counting standards had not rejected ballots containing over votes (where a voter hole-punches multiple candidates but writes out the name of their intended candidate). It should also be noted that the Supreme Court made their decision a one off. That is it did not set precedent, or change legislation.

The Supreme Court of the United States, like all other branches and offices of government, is not perfect. Moreover, SCOTUS has sought to expand its legal powers on par with the ever-expanding authority of Congress and the President. In order to keep up with the other two branches increasing authority, the Court has been, arguably, forced to pursue the same course. Then again, one can argue that the Court, having been established as an apolitical and neutral branch of government, has the responsibility to maintain that neutrality in order to halt the advancing power of the Executive and Legislature. The quote of; "Absolute power corrupts absolutely" would seem to apply to all three branches of the U.S. government. Their constant competition with one another and their headlong pursuit of power expansion has resulted in a government, legal system, and Court, that is increasingly distrusted by the people they are meant to serve. Nonetheless the Court has displayed a tendency through the last half-century to promote individual privacy and freedoms. More often than not it has stood by individuals who sought independence from their state governments, from religious institutions, and even from family ties. The court's power is expansive but on the balance it seems to use that power to promote the rights of individuals to choose their own paths. That's a version of governance which is tolerable.

Recommended further reading

The Supreme Court by William Rehnquist

http://www.supremecourt.gov/

The Constitution of the United States of

America History in Quotations

http://www.supremecourthistory.org/

About the Author

Chris Bartlett spent several years teaching Chinese adults and college students how to speak English and understand American culture. Many of his students were passionately curious about the American political system, having been told not to think about their own system for much of their lives. Answering their questions and constructing lesson plans around the American democratic process left Chris with a surfeit of facts that are only useful once every four years.

Having left his teaching career behind him and returning to America, Chris was surprised to discover that his fellow Americans often had only a marginally more comprehensive understanding of the political processes than did his Chinese students. This has led Chris to be an annoying know-it-all at parties who has heard the admonishment "You should write a book!" one too many times.

He now lives in Colorado with a Chihuahua named Sophia.

www.ingramcontent.com/pod-product-compliance
Lightning Source LLC
Chambersburg PA
CBHW081231280526
45787CB00006B/2606